KU-250-765

Contents

I would especially like to thank Uncle Dec, without whom this book would have been much more difficult to write and a good deal less amusing.

Maria Luisa Palumbo

New Wombs

Electronic Bodies and Architectural Disorders

Birkhäuser – Publishers for Architecture
Basel • Boston • Berlin

Translation into English: Lucinda Byatt. Edit

A CIP catalogue record for this book is available from the Library of Congress, Washington D.C., USA.

Deutsche Bibliothek Cataloging-in-Publication Data

Palumbo, Maria Luisa:
New wombs : electronic bodies and architectural disorders / Maria Luisa Palumbo.
[Transl. into Engl.: Lucinda Byatt]. - Basel ; Boston ; Berlin : Birkhäuser, 2000
(The IT revolution in architecture)
Einheitssacht.: Nuovi ventri <engl>
ISBN 3-7643-6294-4

Original edition:
Nuovi ventri. Corpi elettronici e disordini architettonici (Universale di Architettura 87, collana fondata da Bruno Zevi; La Rivoluzione Informatica, sezione a cura di Antonino Saggio).
© 2000 Testo & Immagine, Turin

© 2000 Birkhäuser – Publishers for Architecture, P.O. Box 133, CH-4010 Basel, Switzerland.
Printed on acid-free paper produced of chlorine-free pulp. TCF ∞
Printed in Italy
ISBN 3-7643-6294-4

9 8 7 6 5 4 3 2 1

Towards a Postorganic Paradigm

The belly, the mysterious place where life takes shape, has been opened to the world. Today it symbolises a radically new concept of the body, characterised by an unprecedented continuity between exterior and interior because, when the naked eye can go no further, artificial sight takes over, revealing life's most intimate and secret aspects.

An instrument of this new continuity between surface and depth, the *machine* leads our eyes and our senses into our body, to the depths of our planet or onto the moon. From being an instrument of alterity between nature and artifice, it has now become the tool for a new dialogue between men, and between man and matter, between man and nature. Dialogue narrows and even eliminates distance, transforming alterity into convergence.

While the body, invaded and dilated by technology becomes architecture, architecture in turn looks to the body, not as a model of order and formal measurement, but as a model of sensitivity, flexibility, intelligence and communicative capacity. Whereas the body designs its own spatial extension, architecture designs its corporeal future.

The new convergence between body and architecture through electronic technology is described as *postorganic*. Our horizon is characterised by a paradigmatic reversal of perspective, making it essential to overcome the logic of opposition between the *organic* universe of the body and the *mechanical* universe of technology, in a new logic of complexity in which the life of the body and forms meet through the machine.

The word machine is used here to denote a symbolic value that, at this time of revolution, underlines the importance of a diachronic point of view to understand the role played by technique in the relationship between the body and architecture. A continuous thread binds (and opposes) the perspective machine and the electronic machine as *strategies of vision*, in other words, intermediate instruments between the *body and space* in understanding and depicting reality.

In the following pages, this discussion of the relationships between the body, architecture and the computer revolution is divided into three parts.

The first, *the dismeasurable body*, reconstructs the gradual transformation of the corporeal model as a paradigm of architecture from the modern age to the present. The aim is to understand how different *ideas of the body* give rise to different ways of relating the body to architecture, arriving at the hypothesis of a new tension towards a form of convergence between the morphological principles of architecture and the body as a *living system*.

The project of chaos suggests a second approach that, moving in space rather than in time, reviews architectural research in the eighties and nineties in order to highlight aspects linked to the difficulty of *measuring* the contemporary body. Countless lines of research are presented, centred on at least two key questions. While architecture as the design of a definite and delimited *object* sees the body as a model of *dismeasurement*, the deconstruction of the certainty and solidity of form, the same formal question tends to dissolve when the object disappears from the network of *interconnections* and the project's tendency to elaborate the limits between physical and telematic space, the elaboration of a new *in-between* zone between nature and artifice, the body and the built-up surface, the surface as the limit of space and the *hypersurface* as a window onto the world of *interactions*.

The logic of complexity is the last step that completes the circle. While the more daring frontier of new relations between the body and architecture aspires towards a *sensitisation* of space, namely architecture's aspiration to *be embodied* or to acquire awareness through electronics, an ulterior radical transformation of the machine appears to lie at the root of this possibility.

In order to translate the sensitive architecture of the living body into new *intelligent* spaces, the information paradigm must be changed from the mechanical and computational logic of the *abstract* machine into a logic of visual and metaphorical complexity, the logic that underlies the physical or *corporeal* basis of living systems. This transition appears to be the key to the conception of a new hybrid tool, capable of mediating the information codes of the body and technology.

1. The Dismeasurable Body

1.1 The Man in the Circle

In the third book of *De Architettura*, dedicated to the sacred architecture of temples, Vitruvius starts by describing the proportions of the human figure as the model for architectonic proportions. The harmony of the body is in turn guaranteed by the geometric harmony of the perfect figures of the circle and the square, into which the human figure, with its splayed arms and legs, fits perfectly.

It is well known that Vitruvius's work contains no images and the graphic interpretation of his descriptions were a major source of inspiration for Renaissance treatises. But this transition, this translation between two worlds, two ages and two different languages, affirms something new and revolutionary.

The problem of the body's measurement, or the body as a model of measurement, shifts from the demonstration of its correct dimensions to a demonstration of the *commensurability* of man and space, between the subjective order of the body and the objective, mathematical and necessary order of natural or celestial harmony.

This is highlighted by Leonardo's interpretation of the Vitruvian 9 figure. The object of the image is clearly stated: the human figure placed in a circle and a square. But Leonardo makes at least three crucial choices. He draws a clear distinction between the pure and adimensional outline of geometry and the restless and expressive outline of the body (its muscles, wrinkles and hair). He differentiates the centres of the square and the circle, thus underlining the individual character of the figures and creating a strained balance between them. When the geometric figure is doubled in size, he doubles the size of the human figure (positioning the limbs on orthogonal and diagonal axes to show the precise and univocal correspondence between the dimensions of the body in both positions and the dimensions of the two figures). The space of the body coincides exactly with the space common to the two figures, thereby reinforcing the dynamic balance of the whole.

The theme of the drawing is clearly no longer merely the harmonious proportions of the body, but the search for a higher level of harmony, one that guarantees to solve the contrast between two orders or opposite signs: the objectivity of numbers, law and measurement and the subjectivity of the body, sight and the human being. The comparison between an absolute and universal geometry and the geometry of ephemeral, vulnerable, relative flesh: the proof of a harmony that resolves the clash between the individual dimension of conscience and the collective dimension of reason and science.

This is the gap that separates Leonardo from Vitruvius, the problem that provided the basis but also tormented the modern age: the question of turning measurement into method, transforming the beauty of the body, as a harmony susceptible to demonstration, from the model of the work to a guarantee for the principles to be applied.

This is the corporeal basis of the *perspective paradigm*: the body as a system of measurement looks onto the world through mathematical eyes in a gaze that translates the immediacy of individual impression into a proportional view that rationalises vision and makes it an *instrument of scientific inquiry*, an instrument for the exact representation of reality.

This is the corporeal basis of art, thought and modern science, the idea of a principle of objectivity inscribed in the heart of subjectivity. A principle of order and rationality that affirms and exalts the individual dimension that protects it.

When directly included in architectonic form, the human figure becomes the guarantor of a harmony that is independent of subjective perception, a mathematical and necessary harmony, one that can be demonstrated and is universally valid, that authorises and legitimises individual creativeness, freedom of research and expression.

This conception of the body as a model of commensurability between the human microcosm and the divine macrocosm is the fulcrum of Renaissance aesthetics and architecture.

1.2 The Eyes of Olympia: the Body as a Machine of the Senses

Renaissance artists were convinced that an innate or instinctive sentiment would allow man to become tuned with the

THE BODY AS A UNIT OF MEASUREMENT

By matching the dimensions of the body with the perfect dimensions of the circle and square, the Vitruvian Figure lays the foundations for Renaissance aesthetics, legitimising the commensurability *of the subjective order of the body and the objective, mathematical and necessary order of natural or celestial harmony.*

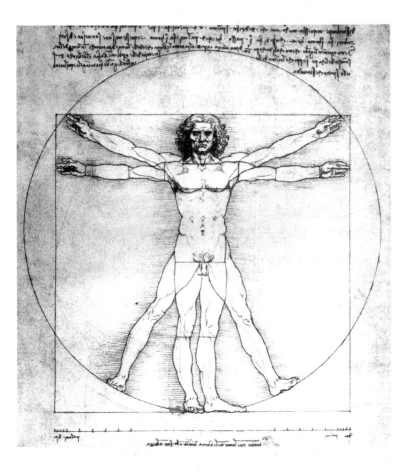

Leonardo, Vitruvian figure, *c. 1490.*

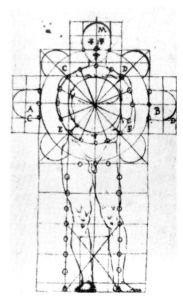

Left: Francesco di Giorgio, Study of proportions. *Right: Francesco di Giorgio,* Example of church with composite plan.

The human figure inscribed in the architectural form guarantees a harmony that was independent of subjective perception: a mathematical and necessary harmony that was demonstrable and universally valid.

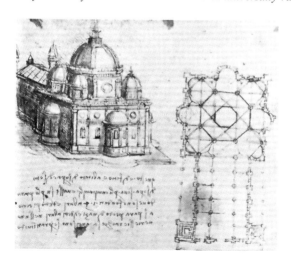

Leonardo da Vinci, Project for a church with a composite *plan.*

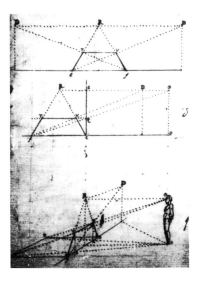

The body as a system of measurement looks onto the world through mathematical eyes in a gaze that translates the immediacy of individual impression into a proportional view that rationalises vision and makes it an instrument of scientific inquiry, *an instrument for the exact representation of reality.*

Left: Ludovico Cardi, Treatise of practical perspective, *1628.*

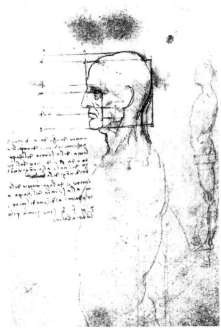

Right: Leonardo da Vinci, Study of proportions.

proportions of a space that formed part of the universal harmony.

But this certainty was gradually undermined by a radically different feeling, based on suppositions that were implicit in the very strategies that had founded modernity. In the same way as the rigid perspective view converging on an unattainable vanishing point had opened a slit, a fissure revealing an unexplored figurative potential (that of perspective as a trick of illusion and the curved line as a deviation from rationality), Cartesian dualism between the thinking element and the body element, its postulation of the body's autonomy as a machine or organ of the senses, indirectly opened the way to a new logic of the body as the *logic of the senses*.

The inability of the eye "to see all three dimensions at the same time and in a single glance" (Temanza) and therefore to perceive the harmony of the proportional ratios of a space, was the first argument that opposed proportional aesthetics from a completely new point of view. The eye replaced reason; the organ of sense, the capacity to understand.

The objective dimensions of harmony were undermined by the subjective reality of perception: the perfect and absolute nature of proportions was opposed by their relative nature, judged on the basis of the effective observation of space using precise angles of visibility.

The idea of the body as a model of formal measurement was replaced by the idea of the body as a *system of perception*. This led to the conviction that architectural forms should be concordant with the laws of the senses rather than the proportions of the body.

After the works by the Italians Scamozzi, Temanza, Guarini and Milizia, it was in England during the course of the eighteenth century that the foundations of Renaissance aesthetics were finally overturned.

Hogarth's *Analysis of Beauty* refuted the principle of correspondence between mathematics and beauty; Hume's *Dissertation on the Standard of Taste* argued that beauty was not a quality of the object, affirming that beauty or any other

THE BODY AS A MACHINE OF THE SENSES

During the 16th and 17th centuries the journeys of exploration and colonisation, the division of the church and the Copernican revolution led to the disintegration of the harmonious Renaissance universe and prompted a completely new vision of the world and man. The visual machine was turned into a scenic machine, an instrument of the possible and the marvellous.

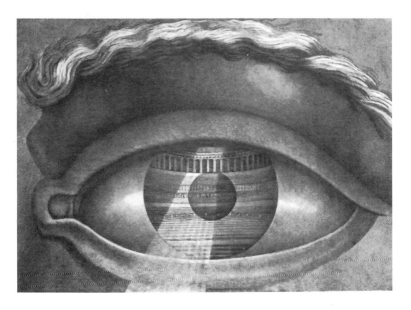

Claude Nicholas Ledoux, Theatre at Besançon, *1780.*

sentiment belonged to the sensitivity of the subject; Burke's *Philosophical Inquiry into the Origin of our Ideas of the Sublime and the Beautiful* laid the basis for a new aesthetics of incommensurability, of revelation that was dazzling, distressing and visionary.

The *rebel line* that escaped the order of pure reason in search of emotion and sentiment (the line that, having been the predominant feature of the Baroque, was responsible for both

14

The idea of the body as a model of formal measurement was replaced by the idea of the body as a system of perception. *Reason was replaced by the eye; the capacity to understand by the organ of sense. This led to the conviction that architectural forms should be concordant with the laws of the senses rather than the proportions of the body.*

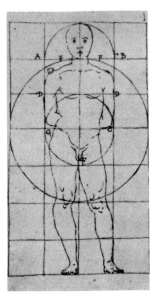

Right: Francesco di Giorgio, Example of church with central plan.

Left: René Descartes, Treatise on man. *Facing page: Fritz Lang,* Metropolis, *1927.*

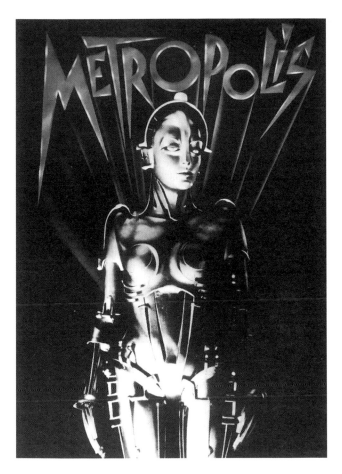

Whereas the machine of visual perspective had radicalised alterity and the hierarchy between the subject and object of vision, the appearance of the artificial eye not only overturned the concept of the machine (from an instrument to look through to an instrument through which you could be seen), but also the general horizon of sight. Man and machine now looked at each other. Leaving aside the fears and desires of the collective imagination, the underlying question was not the disappearance of the differences, but rather the new compatibility, a revolutionary convergence between technology and biology.

the dissolution of rationalism in visionary research and the dissolution of Neoclassicism through the picturesque), became the undisputed protagonist in the aesthetics of *Einfühlung*. This gave the line, and the type of energy and sensation that it generated, the capacity for the form to directly influence the body's psychic states.

Shortly after the publication of Sigmund Freud's *The Interpretation of Dreams*, Henry Van de Velde proclaimed the existence of a silent dialogue between the restless *lay lines* crossing through space and the psychic life of the body. In *Abstraktion und Einfühlung*, Wilhelm Worringer attributed the tendency to use abstract geometric forms and natural organic forms to a single psychological matrix, explaining it as the dual requirement of the human spirit.

Therefore, between the late nineteenth century and early twentieth century the idea of the body as a system of perception gave way to that of the body as a *psychophysical system*, and the principle of formal correspondence and sensitive agreement was replaced by the idea of an intimate and suffered correspondence between organic and inorganic forms of a sexual, relative, heterogeneous and unstable universe. The perceptive reading of the eye was replaced by a new semantic and psychological reading of architecture.

Walter Benjamin is responsible for the critical intuition that suggested seeing the characteristic lines of art nouveau as a synthesis of the modern electric wires and nerves: a new *symbolic form* of contact between the organic world and technique, between the turbulence of the neurovegetative system and the most radical discovery of his era, electricity. Benjamin was firmly convinced that, rather than a contact, this was a reciprocal dissolution: he identified Olympia, the *automaton* who plays the leading role in a story by E.T.A. Hoffmann, as the ideal woman of art nouveau, built to dissolve the distinction between technology and biology.

Whereas the machine of visual perspective had radicalised alterity and the hierarchy between the subject and object of vision, the appearance of the *artificial eye* not only overturned the concept of the machine (from an instrument to look through to an instrument through which you could be seen), but also the general horizon of sight. Man and machine now look at each other.

Leaving aside the fears and desires of the collective imagination, the underlying question is not the disappearance of the differences, but rather the new compatibility, a revolutionary convergence between technology and biology.

1.3 Space with Figures: the Body in Prosthesis

Bauhaus's peculiarity lies in its nature as a polyvalent workshop. This transversal nature finds a legitimate living space in the art of performance. Theatre and dance, stage and body, image and word, sound and light, everything finds its own place in a new provocative dissolution of expressive genres. But while performance is already a creation of our contemporary age, of which it reflects all the features (from the centrality of the body to the breaking down of closed art forms), the uniqueness of Bauhaus's performance is the clarity with which it became a tool for exploring the new mechanical space through a *bio-mechanical body*.

A body that becomes a meeting ground for technology and biology.

By embodying the artificial nature of the mechanical universe, Schlemmer's puppet bodies move in search of new possibilities for relationships, among what appeared to be irremediably opposing terms, experimenting a path of promiscuous intimacy that modernism had inaugurated on an abstract symbolic plane. The body *becomes a machine* through a stage costume that is a mechanised system of parts, as is unequivocally declared by the title of the performances, starting with *Metallic Festival* and later *Dance of Glass*, *Metallic Ballet*, and *Man + Machine*.

But what is the link between the complicated superstructures of Schlemmer's costumes and the aerial transparency of Gropius's architecture?

The body that appears on stage is a body *extended through space*, a body where costume and scenery merge, where anatomic and spatial geometric forms become a single form

THE BODY IN PROSTHESIS

The body that the Bauhaus theatrical laboratory placed on stage is a body extended through space, a body where costume and scenery merge, where anatomic and spatial geometric forms become a single form of nature and culture. A mechanical body, a meeting ground for technology and biology.

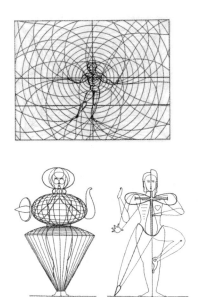

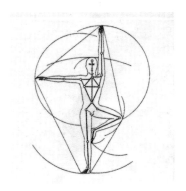

Top and left: Oskar Schlemmer, Studies for stage costumes, *c. 1921. Bottom: Oskar Schlemmer,* Triadic ballet, *1926.*

of nature and culture. In the same way, the invention of a code that enabled glass to be handled, not merely as stone had been handled for thousands of years, but with all the new possibilities offered by the material, permitted the artifice of a wall reduced to a thin blade of light. Namely a surface that joins rather than divides, *opening up* the interior space to the world and its constant variability (in terms of atmosphere, light, landscape), opening the way for a new trend in architecture towards the *flexibility* of organic forms.

Therefore, the mechanical strategy announced its revolution through the biomechanical body of Bauhaus and its light space: it is possible to extend the body, to sensitise space.

In some ways (by making improper use of the expression to describe architecture in the age of the machine), this is the core problem of the *machine à habiter*. To establish a dialogue between the body and space, in a new form of *prosthetic architecture*, or in other words an architecture that replaces the need for official representation with the basic requisites of living, the quality of *existenz minimum*, light, air, hygiene for all and physical wellbeing as the basis for psychic equilibrium.

Ergonomics and psychofunctionalism are merely different responses to the same problem: namely the new centrality of the body, its forms, its measurements, its needs, its instincts.

But from the point of view of the body, the more clearly differentiated the paths taken by research, the clearer it is that they share a common root. This is the reason why living space, the central architectural theme of the 20th century, which is also the one closest to the human body, has evolved in two divergent directions.

The *sanatorium* house, with its roof garden for sunbathing and physical exercise, raised on pilotis above the humidity and impurities of the ground, and built and furnished to suit the measurements of the body. And the *womb* or shell house, with its organic and enveloping cavity which opposes the aesthetics of sun and light with the sensual, protective and dark visceral nature of the cave, a return to the earth, to formless matter, to natural *folds* rather than straight angles and orthogonal surfaces.

In some ways this is the core problem of the machine à habiter. *Establishing a dialogue between the body and space, in a new form of* prosthetic architecture, *or in other words an architecture which replaces the need for official representation with the basic requisites of living, the quality of* existenz minimum, *the new centrality of the body, its forms, its measurements, its needs, its instincts.*

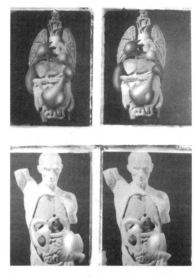

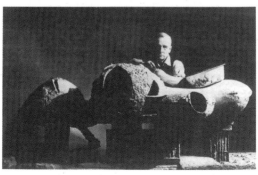

Top: Nat Chard, Architecture of our interior, *1995. Bottom: Frederick Kiesler,* Endless House, *model exhibited in New York in 1960. Facing page: Francis Bacon,* Portrait of George Dyer talking, *1966.*

Le Corbusier's modular and measured bodies and Kiesler's body, which is obsessively attached to his Endless House, *express a radical break. Precisely the extensibility of the body, its extreme possibilities of dislocation in time and space result in the explosion of the box, the final disappearance of a concept of identity based on a single and univocal model of the body.*

In this sense, the modulor *represents the last attempt to stop the collapse, to reaffirm the principle of the Vitruvian figure: the human figure as an element of certainty, an objective and unchanging measurement on which to base a legitimate and univocal criterion of design.*

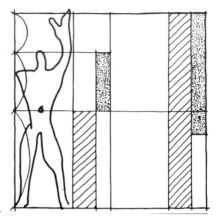

Le Corbusier, Modulor, *1942-1948.*

The new technique of reinforced concrete and skills in the handling of steel and bending wood help to fulfil and stimulate both fields of research.

The contraposition lies upstream from the architectural forms.

It is a contrast of bodies, or rather corporeal models. The athletic, sporting, muscular, healthy body shining under the sun of the *new spirit* is contrasted with a *new body*, a body that has lost the certainty of ego, an unstable, restless, unbalanced and instinctive body.

Seen in these terms, while Schlemmer's puppet-like bodies express a new extensibility, Le Corbusier's modular bodies and Kiesler's body, which is obsessively attached to his *Endless House*, express a radical break.

The extensibility of the body, its total world availability in the global village of communications, its extreme possibilities of dislocation in time and space result in the *explosion of the box*, the final disappearance of a concept of identity based on a single and univocal model of the body.

In this sense, the *modulor* represents the last attempt to stop the collapse, to reaffirm the principle of the Vitruvian figure:

the human figure as an element of certainty, an objective and unchanging measurement on which to base a legitimate and univocal criterion for relations between man and the world.

As became evident during the course of the century, in the *era of infinite possibilities*, the body has become the measurement of a continuous drive to *overstep the limits*, a constant tension to *surpass* all measures. From being the centre of a proportional system with all things, it has become an anthropological measurement of the deconstruction of every presumed *principle of reality*.

1.4 The Cyborg: the Body without Organs

After the end of metaphysics and the death of the gods, another fall is being prepared at the start of another millennium, another disappearance.

Under the sign of the body, our century started with the urgent need to bare the skin, to open up the flesh, to travel through the deliria of the brain. Its closing years saw the attempt to move *beyond the body* and its physical nature, to embody the projections of a virtual world and to explore the potential of a *postorganic* body.

This is the phenomenon of the hybridisation of the body and technology: working in both directions of technology grafted onto the organic body and the dissemination of the body through telematic networks.

This is *cyborg*, the technologically extended organism: the body that ends at the furthest point of the radius of action of its sensors and remote-control devices, linking biological rhythms and a media universe crossed by information flows.

This is no alien or replicated body, but instead a new "appearance of our incarnation" (Haraway 95), providing constant and continuous contact with the world. Contact that is no longer simply that with the ground on which we rest our feet, but on the contrary, contact that stems from our possible emancipation from geophysical constraints.

The body, having been stripped, opened, disembowelled, is now dilated, transformed and reconfigured.

Stelarc, an Australian performer is convinced of the body's

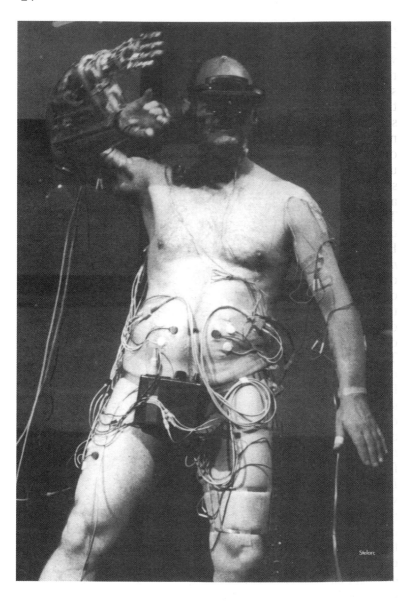

Stelarc, Amplified Body, *1986.*

non-actuality. Since the seventies he has explored the functions, limits and possibilities of his body. After the so-called *suspension events* (suspended in galleries or open spaces by ropes ending in hooks embedded in the flesh), Stelarc has started to redesign the body to increase its cybernetic potential, using mechanical prostheses, like the *third hand* (linked to sensors positioned on other areas of the body which emit signals that are electrically associated to the various movements of the artificial limb), and even more radical internal reconfigurations, like the *sculpture for stomach* (a miniaturised capsule with a TV camera that, having been swallowed, opens and starts to bleep and flash when it reaches the stomach). The artist gives a clear-cut picture of the horizons of what he defined as "post-evolution strategies".

Electronic space will develop increasingly rapidly from *information media* to a *space for action*. Along the way, the body's operational parameters will no longer be limited by its physiology or its immediate surroundings. Remote operation systems make it possible to project the human presence over distances, achieving an ubiquity that will allow them to carry out physical actions even in extraterrestrial locations.

Thus, while "the most significant event in the history of our evolution has been the change in the mode of locomotion, future developments will require a change of skin." The construction of a synthetic skin, "capable of absorbing oxygen directly through its pores and converting light into nutritious chemical substances" will make it possible to "*redesign the body*, eliminating many of its superfluous systems and malfunctioning organs."

Leaving aside Stelarc's provocative predictions, in the real world, apart from commonly used technological appendices (like mobile phones and other portable electronic systems, contact lenses, dentures, etc.), the continuity and collaboration between the body and electronic technology plays an essential role in the rehabilitation of increasingly severe *disabilities*, using solutions that are grafted more and more intimately into the patient's body.

Hearing aids, consisting of chips implanted in the inner ear,

THE BODY WITHOUT ORGANS

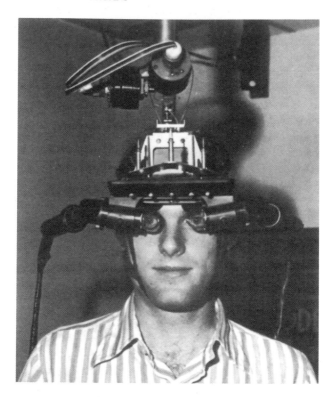

In the era of limitless possibilities, the body becomes a measure of excess, a measure of the possibility of going beyond the body and its physical limitations. This is the phenomenon of the hybridisation of the body and technology: the cyborg, the technologically extended organism that links biological rhythms and a media universe crossed by information flows. But the most powerful translation that electronics allows is not that of a virtual body, but rather that of a real body through which it is possible to acquire (mediated) experience of every part of the world and universe, the infinitely large and the infinitely small, the infinitely immense times and spaces of the stars and the infinitely minute spaces of atoms. While the rigid and metric logic of perspective allowed the profundity of the world to be reduced to a single plane, to lead the multitude of points to a single vanishing point, and the variety of elements to a single scale of comparison, the liquid *nature of digital information now allows us to dialogue with the most secret and vital aspects of nature, leading to the jagged measurement of clouds and mountains, the* dynamic, flexible and sensitive *nature of the body as a living system.*

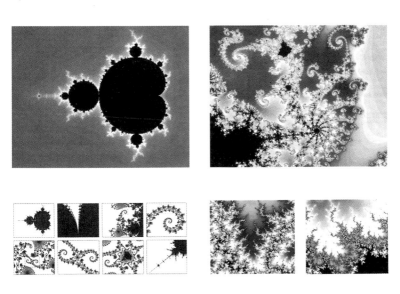

Opposite: top, Ivan Sutherland, prototype of the first virtual reality helmet, 1970; bottom: Stelarc, Amplified Body/Enhanced Image, *1994. This page: image of Mandelbrot's fractal (taken from the programme* PowerXplorer *by Alessandro Levi Montalcini, 1994).*

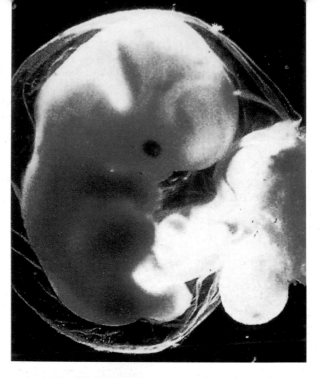

The transition from the idea of the body as a biomechanical system to the body as a bioelectronic system *delineates the boundary of a relationship of* electromagnetic continuity *between man and space through machines: the possibility of a link or far-reaching convergence no longer between* forms, *but between the* information codes *of architecture and the body as a living system.*

Opposite: top, Embryo in maternal womb; bottom: Astronaut in space. This page: Van Berkel & Box, Real Space in Quick Times Pavilion, *Milan Biennial, 1996.*

process sounds from a microphone positioned behind the ear and translate them into impulses transmitted to the brain by the auditory nerve. Bionic eyes, consisting of miniaturised TV cameras that replace the optic system of the eye and a microchip implanted in the cerebral cortex to act as an artificial retina, transform luminous information into electric signals to be transmitted to the brain. Systems designed to restore motor function in paraplegics will soon be used to forge a direct link between the nervous system and the cybernetic prosthesis, making it possible to command the artificial limb using cerebral impulses.

The possibility of knowing and managing the body's *electric nature* is the underlying factor for a range of instruments designed to enable the neural and body control of computers. The aim is to create an interface that does not require manual control like a mouse or keyboard, but instead relies on connections between the computer's electric circuits and the body's *electric impulses*.

Electric signals emitted by the body which can, to a greater or lesser extent, be controlled by the individual and interpreted by the computer, take the form of electromyographical signals from the muscles, electro-oculographical signals from the eyes and electric signals from the brain. The underlying principle of control is based on the possibility that the subject can learn to alter the *breadth* of these signals.

In practice, there is nothing more artificial in this than the articulated use of fingers, gestures or the voice. In short, it entails exploring a frontier of our body that is still essentially unknown and, in this electronic era, might prove to be radically important.

In fact, in addition to the boundless possibilities offered by mechanical prostheses that could extend the body's physical capabilities and open up new territories, another possibility of extension also involving the exploration of as yet unknown territories, is represented by the bare electric nature of our bodies. *Telematic man* at the end of the millennium can be interpreted in this sense as the same being of flesh and blood, but also a being whose consciousness is linked to his ability to control his own material and electric nature.

The transition from the idea of the body as a *biomechanical system* to the body as a bioelectronic system lies at the cutting edge of a radical leap from an anthropomorphic model of formal correspondence to a new form of relationship or *electromagnetic continuity* between man and space through machines. The criterion of proportional geometry, the sensitive agreement and prosthetic extension appear to be followed by the possibility of a link or far-reaching convergence no longer between forms, but between organisational principles, or between the *information codes* of architecture and the body as a living system.

We can no longer define this convergence as organic because it stems from the body's rebellion against the organism as a closed, univocal and definite form, moving towards a hybrid and transversal nature that eludes Euclidean measurements, the rigid laws of perspective and the logic of *alterity* between organic and inorganic.

While the body now can be integrated indifferently with valves, prostheses, artificial and natural organs, in turn machines not only simulate the structural principles of living systems, but also start to integrate biological matter into their mechanisms.

This far-reaching transversality, the possibility of not only making nature artificial, but also inverting the process by *naturalising the artificial*, is the horizon that the key of the body points to as the new logic for the co-existence of differences in a system of changing, jagged, folded, deformable geography, a system where the possibility of *relation* predominates over the possibility of measurement, where the capacity for *connection* and *interaction* predominates over *formal* definition.

Research in the field of bioelectronic body and rehabilitation for the disabled overlaps with studies for a new environmental sensitivity. In fact, by strengthening and emphasising the demand for intelligent and ecological architecture, capable of lightly skimming over the ground and becoming a *threshold* rather than a barrier, both bodies and landscapes in extreme situations highlight the complex play of forces in space as a political frontier rather than one of form.

2. The Project of Chaos

2.1 Utopia and Chaotic Attractors

The enthusiasm and criticism of the sixties, disaffection for society and euphoria for the burgeoning pop and media universe expressed themselves in a ferment of utopias that saw the analogy between architectural and anatomical structure as a fertile source of metaphors for a new architecture within human grasp.

In the experimental designs put forward by the Viennese groups Haus-Rucker-Co and Coop Himm(l)blau, both the equipment used in space exploration programmes and the more secret internal architecture of the body, together with the forms of its organs and their organisation, became a direct source of inspiration for their architectural proposals.

For the English architects forming part of Archigram, the fundamental principle of living had "to be reconsidered in the light of technological progress and the possibility of increasing personal mobility." In fact, this led to a "rejection of permanence", a growing "curiosity and desire for knowledge: it might lead to a world whose movements resembled the early nomadic societies." As a result, while the parts of Peter Cook's *Plug in City* are mobile, in other words, they can be taken apart and recomposed, the megastructures of Ron Herron's *Walking City* can be moved on telescopic legs or slide along on cushions of air.

The fundamental novelty that emerged from this electronic euphoria, which would find a realistic design formulation in Piano and Roger's proposals for the Pompidou Centre (in particular the elements that were not constructed, like the large electronic screen on the façade and the mobile floors), can be summed up as the possibility of conceiving architecture not as a masonry box (exploded to a greater or lesser degree), but instead as a *sensitive, flexible and modifiable structure*.

Over and above their anatomic or zoomorphic forms, these architectural designs showed attention to renewed discipline, based on an attempt to reproduce the capacity for *communication and dynamic adaptation* characteristic of living beings.

Over the decades that followed, the formal analogy between the profound or anatomic structure of the body and architectural structure would be substantially abandoned in favour of other ways of establishing new relations, whether real or metaphorical, with a body characterised by its fluid form (constantly redesigned using plastic surgery, technological prostheses or telematic digitalisation), and by a growing relationship of electronic continuity with its surroundings.

The body, as the unstable margin between the ego and the world, between the real and the imaginary, or the existing and the project, became a system of *connections* and *interactions*.

A complex system that failed to generate a univocal and determined image or design criteria, but attracted the lines of architectural research around a series of fixed points.

Dismeasurement as the opening, deconstruction or dissemination of the formal identity of an object/project.

Uprooting as the tendency towards deterritorialisation, mobility, temporariness and the precarious nature of equilibrium.

Fluidity as research into the possible dissolution of form into spatial vibration.

A *visceral nature* as the exploration of the limit between formed and formless matter.

Virtuality as extreme dematerialisation, a journey through the multidimensional nature of the adimensional.

Sensitivity as the capacity for relation, perception and interaction.

2.2 Urban Dismeasurement

Jaggedness, a language that describes clouds, irregular geometry and the chaotic dynamics of everything that escapes order, measurement, the gaze and the representation of the territory. A language to open the idea of the city to the qualitative measurement of the body, and architecture to the perceptive exploration of territory. Even before the project, the problem of dismeasurement concerns the overall vision of the city.

It is more difficult to identify the limits of the city (the suburbs that were previously countryside) and the curious pres-

CHAOTIC ATTRACTORS

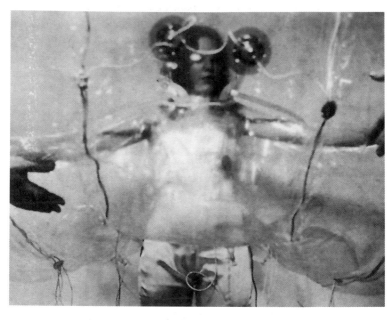

Above: Haus-Rucker-Co, Mind Expander I, *1967. Left: Coop Himm(l)blau,* Heartroom, *1969.*

In the sixties, disaffection for society and euphoria for the burgeoning pop and media universe expressed themselves in a ferment of utopias that saw the analogy between architectural and anatomical structure as a fertile source of metaphors for a new architecture within human grasp. The essential novelty lay in conception of architecture as a sensitive, flexible and modifiable structure. *In the eighties and nineties, the body, as a complex system, failed to generate a univocal and determined image or design criterion, but attracted the lines of architectural research around a series of fixed points linked to the attempt to reproduce the communicative and dynamic co-adaptive capacities of living beings.*

Archigram, Walking City, *1964.*

ence of holes inside the city becomes more evident. Namely, the existence of *internal margins*, changing but often vague boundaries, beyond which you are somewhere else.

The spread of the urban phenomena over an increasingly vast area, in ways that are less closely linked to the territory itself, coupled with other factors like the obsolescence and mobility of the different parts of the city, have given rise to a phenomenon of urban dispersion which has created a special type of refuse, *urban residue*: empty or abandoned buildings, often jumbled together, a hybrid of disused human constructions and the metabolisation of these built-up areas by flora and fauna that are free to reproduce at the very limits of rules and controls.

Compared to this novel suburban context, many have observed the reduced efficacy of the cognitive and design capacity of traditional instruments. The need for a radical renovation of language.

39, 42 *Stalker*, a laboratory of urban art and territorial research, designs and promotes a new idea of the city, comparing the structure of Rome to the fractal structure of galaxies. It takes a few days of uninterrupted "urban drifting" to cross and map these *fractal cities*, following the system of emptiness in its interstitial penetrations and linking in a single walkabout what it defines as "current territories": territories in the process of being transformed, at the limit of measurement, control, discipline, at the limit of turning into *something else*.

What should be done in this context?

Certainly the first thing is to explore it, rather than ignore it. But it is even more important to know how to cross this "reject city", self-built with materials and spaces rejected by the city, overturning its residual nature, bringing light to a territory that is far from empty, absolutely central to the new dynamics of the urban scene. Having blurred the threshold between the city and the non-city, a new threshold emerges within the city, making the city itself a frontier system between worlds whose physical distance is irrelevant because it is divided by the lack of measurement, or the disproportionate gap between wealth and hunger, between peace and war.

Alongside Augé's pervasive *non-places* and Foucault's evasive *counterplaces* (or heterotopies), the jagged identity of *current territories* prompts us to reflect on an emerging urban complexity where the dynamics of the evolution of Western social and manufacturing systems (the *liberation* of industrial areas or historic city centres) are mixed with the dynamics arising from the reconfiguration and political and territorial restructuring of entire geographical areas in the rest of the world (with the consequent *occupation* of our disused territories by populations from the widest range of cultural, political and geographical contexts).

The city must come face to face as soon as possible with this dramatically but also vitally concrete aspect of the global and postcolonial village of the new millennium, where the ideal measurement of the Vitruvian body is deconstructed into a kaleidoscope of different languages and colours.

This is where the limit is, the frontier, the point of imbalance, the pivot for the challenge of new *urban art*: moving beyond the poetic inspiration of land art (the idea of a territorial art rather than a museum art), beyond the situationist criticism of the functional city (the strategies of spatial and conceptual inquiry born from movements for a new antirationalist or *imaginary* Bauhaus), to position the project between *complexity* and *immediacy*, in search of efficacious instruments so that architecture (like science) can start to move alongside (urban) phenomena without suppressing or failing to recognise their dynamic, open, conflictual and heterogeneous nature.

2.3 Architectural Dismeasurement

The dismeasurable nature of a drawing where the loss of the centre (the loss of order, hierarchy, recognition) corresponds to an increasingly inarticulate or jagged confusion of boundary lines is the clearest and most characteristic *attractor* of projects that are sensitive to the new concept of complexity.

In this sense, the technological and megastructural tension of the Archigram designs contained even more important germs than the structures for corporeal stimulation proposed by the Viennese groups.

While the link with the *corporeal aspect* of these machines of

38

desire is even more evident, their evolution can be likened to a gradual reduction of the spatial aspect to a wearable surface, reducing the body-to-body contact between machine and man to an increasingly intimate contact, providing access to a virtual dimension of multisensorial stimulation.

On the contrary, the subversive war machines of the Archigram architects, with their restless mechanical nomadism, move towards a revolutionary concept of architecture that would find a new logic of conformation between landscape and architecture in the unstable, deformable and adaptable geometries of natural forms.

The complexity and flexibility brought about by technology open the way to overcoming the concept of the ground as a tray, to discover the multiple layers, folds and density of the soil, a morphological richness that brings new lymph to the life of the architectural forms.

40, 42 This line of evolution is particularly clear in Peter Cook's drawings and writings. His latest designs reveal the metaphorical disintegration of stratified megastructures which, rather than moving and sliding over the landscape, *dissolve* into it, creating what he calls *melting architecture*.

Natural elements, rocks and vegetation become one with the partially ruined architectural structures under attack, which are also vitally animated by this "nervous" hybridism. Nature and artifice blend, mix, intersect and entangle to form a single, geometrically undefined *jagged landscape* that is out of control, pervaded by a mysterious, wild freedom.

The invasive creatures of the Archigram designs and Cook's metaphorical landscapes find a unique form of development **39, 49** in the architectural rebellion of Lebbeus Woods.

Woods's contestation is total: architecture is an instrument of battle, against power, against gravity, against time, against everything. An architecture that is programmatically anarchic ("Anarchitecture"), a political act of liberation from hierarchy and, in general, liberation from all closures, all determinations of form and substance. Architecture as an instrument of cultural, social and political revolution.

The spaces of Woods's turbulence fill the *free zones* of the city,

DISMEASUREMENT

The opening, deconstruction or dissemination of the formal identity of the project, in a drawing where the loss of centre corresponds to an increasingly inarticulate or jagged confusion of boundary lines, is the clearest and most characteristic attractor *of the design studies sensitive to the new concept of complexity.*

Stalker, Territori attuali. *Lebbeus Woods,* Turbulence Structure, *1991.*

Top: Peter Cook, Way Out West Berlin, *1988. Bottom: Zaha Hadid,* Peak Club, *Hong Kong, 1982-83.*

Marcos Novak, Warp Map, interior, *1988.*

temporarily autonomous zones like the abandoned underground of Berlin, or the sky over Paris.

The project was first created in Berlin in 1988 and stemmed from the desire to cross over the Wall and to set up an underground community in the abandoned areas of the metropolis. An underground and undivided Berlin, one that could escape from authority and control, slipping in between the layers of ground and emerging with disturbing telescopic towers into the sunlight and in full view of the city.

In Paris, the strategy of tension was flanked by one of fascination: from the bottom of the old city, the aerial houses looked like an extravagant gypsy campsite which was both worrying and intriguing at the same time, with its irregular freedom of movement, unregulated by the law and by gravity.

Top: Peter Cook, Way Out West Berlin, *1988. Bottom: Stalker,* Territori Attuali.

If the invasion in the Archigram projects appeared to arrive from space, a far-off, extraterrestrial space inhabited by UFOs and spaceships, here the invasion came from earth. Woods presents us with the *organless body* of the city, a challenge to the organism, the organisation of design *imposed* on the territory.

Woods's architectural utopia is not only deconstructed, but topologically reinscribed in the folds of the earth, the broken outline of the mountains, the fluid metamorphosis of clouds. This utopia is founded on the image and the ungrammatical and distorted strength of the shanty town, the minimum degree of syntax and the maximum capacity for self-construction. The prevalence of dismeasurement over measurement, free deformation over typology: the loss of the centre and boundaries in a single *jagged design*.

In a different way, although forming part of a similar logic, in Zaha Hadid's designs and projects architecture and nature become a single line of strength, a single darting, fleeing landscape whose transformation cannot be stopped.

Nature and artifice, intervention and context, urban velocity and buildings, the whole is bound or rather flows in a continuous broken or jagged line that fills all the gaps, all the possible spaces *between* objects.

While the design for Peak Club in Hong Kong is dominated 40 by the technique of *layering*, the stratification, superimposition and accumulation of successive layers laid on top of one another to replace the soil removed from the side of the hill and form a new geology, in the project for Carnuuntum 44 Museum in Vienna the amphitheatre represents the real declaration of the idea: "architecture as an extension of the landscape" (through the disarticulation of artificial platforms following the trend of the contours), and the belvedere reveals its mechanism of strength: "the jagged forms of the eroded rock wall are artificially reinforced to the utmost limit."

The project line, as an interpretation of the lay lines crossing through space, traces the tension, the erosive or disruptive energy, a perennial flow of natural and artificial forces that prevents the stability of equilibrium.

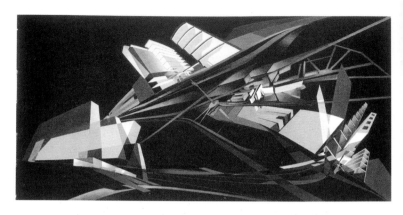

Zaha Hadid: top, Zolhof Media Park, *Dusseldorf, 1993-95; bottom:* Carnuuntum Museum, *Vienna, 1993.*

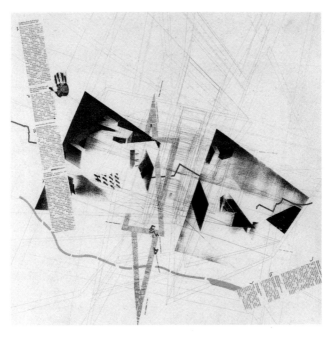

Daniel Libeskind: top, Between the Lines, Star Matrix, *Jewish Museum, Berlin, 1997; bottom:* Extension of the Victoria and Albert Museum, *London, 1996-2001.*

Imbalance, dismeasurement or jaggedness are certainly the attractors of Daniel Libeskind's research.

His projects show a world of multifaceted, changing crystals, superimposed in a precarious equilibrium, forming complex and unpredictable gemmations. However they are read, whether as townscapes or landscapes, the image is that of a chaotic superimposition of heterogeneous elements, accumulated into a original form of *decollage*, projects of exceptional *density* and depth, stratified like the sections of an archeological dig.

The integrity of the work, like that of the city, is in jeopardy, abandoned not only in the substance of the project, but also in its graphic reproduction which breaks down, projects and overlaps the parts in every direction. It is difficult to orientate yourself, to understand the direction, the right way up, the wrong way up, the way in, the way out, the beginning, the end. Images, sketches, fragments of city, writing, notes, newspaper scraps, oriental letters, lists of words and numbers, musical scores, staves: the project seems to be adrift in this sea of relics. But reality is this mass of lines, marks, scars, fractures. And the project must work on these lines, amplifying them into a serious game of cross-references between the visible and the invisible, "what is not shown" must structure and provide the constructive logic for the visible. What cannot be seen is first and foremost the memory, like a profound event, a dramatic fact that is never consolatory.

And memory, the painful memory of the Holocaust is the theme of the Jewish Museum extension to the Berlin
45 Museum. The project, which is entitled *Between the lines* and drawn on a pentagram, is formed by the intersection of two lines: a continuous, twisting, deformed reference to the Star of David, following the winding museum itinerary, and a straight line broken into numerous fragments of pure, empty space. While the entrance to the museum leads down into the depths of the underground, the whole itinerary continues to converge on the depth of the empty space around which it moves, whereas the openings to the outside and the city are merely sharp, thin slits.

2.4 Uprooting

While the Modern Movement was obsessed by the problem of rationalising urban form, today it is precisely its labyrinthine, dynamic and chaotic nature that is most fascinating: the constant movement of persons, things, information and continuous changes in balances and configurations through the superimposition of new layers, new stages and new uses of space.

One of the most surprising aspects of our modern world is that space, rather than being inhabited, seems to exist to be travelled through. Rather than establishing roots, society or societies are broken up, mixed, crossed and uprooted. Out of necessity or curiosity, because of hunger or concern. Owing to a lack or abundance of resources, being homeless or in order to leave home, there is an unending buzz of movement, telephone calls, e-mails. The infrastructures used for these tangible or intangible crossings multiply in terrestrial or celestial space. The *nodes*, the waiting spaces, the areas for rest, meeting, entering and leaving the network, starting and ending a journey spread, multiply and are perfected alongside the *networks*. It is these, without doubt, that are the real focus of the contemporary world, a restless existence on the move.

Increasingly often these are the loci for public life, or for a semi-public, semi-private life, *places of interchange* between people, goods and means of communication. This explains why malls, airports and motorway services are equipped to offer services linked to their new urban function. Meeting places for a deterritorialised but connected society.

"My name is *wjm@mit.edu* (although I have many other aliases) and I am an electronic flâneur. I live in the net." This is how Mitchell starts his book *City of Bits*. He continues by stating that his name-address corresponds to a vague place. As he says, the network is "all around, nowhere particular and not least everywhere." But how can we respond in architectural terms to the nomadism of the body? How can the *project* include the instability, worry and animation that characterise space in the electronic era?

The idea of the precarious or temporary nature of balance and structures is the distinguishing feature of an architecture that

48

While the Modern Movement was obsessed by the problem of rationalising urban form, today it is precisely its labyrinthine, dynamic and chaotic nature that is most fascinating: the constant movement of persons, things, information and continuous changes in balances and configurations through the superimposition of new layers, new stages and new uses of space.

Right: Rem Koolhaas, Villa Dall'Alva, Paris, 1985–1991. *Bottom: Coop Himmelb(l)au, attic in Vienna.*

Lebbeus Woods, Zagreb Free Zone, *1991.*

50

In uprooting the form from stability and traditional order in search of a state of indefiniteness, a form in the process of becoming or on the point of mutating, changing axis, dilating, folding, liquefying, we find a profoundly dynamic concept of the body.

Top: Nomad camp. *Bottom and opposite: Toyo Ito,* PAO2 Dwelling for Tokyo Nomad Woman, *1989.*

The electronic house takes on the character of a nomad's tent: the PA02 Dwelling for Tokyo Nomad Woman *installation is an egg, a shell and a tent to carry round the world in a journey shared by body and architecture.*

has decided to position itself in a radical *threshold condition*, to uproot itself both from the earth and from the discipline.

The strategy is to break down, to disassemble, to lose the whole nature of construction; this does not entail disassembling the traditional elements before re-using them in contemporary architecture, but, on the contrary, a radical opposition of the very tradition of building, unhinging the *certainties* of architecture, the concepts of foundation, finality, and hierarchy. This explains why in the projects by Coop Himme(l)blau, Woods, Hadid, Koolhaas and others, the relationship between building and ground is complicated, the building refuses to take root, it rebels against the laws of gravity, it collapses and breaks up, recomposes into precarious equilibriums, in a form ready to change again, centreless, without an axis perpendicular to the ground or an evident order between the parts, a continuous challenge to the formal and structural capacities of materials, because a *secret perspective is hidden on high*, the inebriation of flight is hidden by the vertigo of the fall.

What should we think of the crystalline silhouette perched
48 like a strange bird on the roof of Coop Himme(l)blau, except that it might take wing at any moment? The extreme incarnation is obtained by wavering the boundaries: instead of an unstable form, this is a form *in the process of becoming*, or *on the point of* mutating, changing axis, dilating, folding, liquefying. The dynamism of the body is translated into the uprooting of the form from stability and traditional order in search of a state of indefiniteness and transformation.

50-51 The architectural research of Toyo Ito is extremely sensitive to the problem of real and virtual nomadism in our contemporary age. Transition, the mobility of people, things, and information are in Ito's opinion the most important factors and therefore the key design stimulus today.

While architecture must explore the possibility of becoming a *filter*, a surface on which to display the migratory flows that cross the media universe (this is the purpose of his *Tower of Winds*, a structure that lives off the flows of information, light, sound and atmosphere that cross through it, provoking changes in its brilliance), the main problem facing dwellings is that of finding a form suited to their temporariness. The electronic house takes on the character of a nomad's tent: the *PA02 Dwelling for Tokyo Nomad Woman* installation is an egg, a shell and a tent to carry round the world in a journey shared by body and architecture.

2.5 Fluidity

It is impossible to doubt the importance of the conceptual hinterland in which Eisenman's architecture has always been rooted. Therefore, while the horizon of rationalism, formally disputed on the edge of a dangerous implosion, takes form in the paper matter of the first series of houses (sufficiently demonstrative, analytical and theoretical to be defined as "cardboard architecture"), the horizon of a radical deconstruction of an equilibrium and an entirety that have lost their raison d'être takes form through laborious excavations, digging up the memory and ground to unearth traces, fragments of lost or potential geometric forms.

In this psychoanalytical terrain, the machine begins to take shape as an instrument to voice rediscovered wishes or, rather, to embody the unstable and metaphorical nature of desires, above all that of being animated by immobile matter.

But in this *logic of transformation* (the transformation of waves and the mark they leave on the beach onto which the "Casa Guardiola" faces, itself a metaphor of that undulatory 55 organic movement), in this logic of a new aesthetics of desire rooted in digital technology (otherwise the Boolean and topological deformations in which this architecture takes form would be inconceivable), in this logic of cosmic feeling that vibrates through the matter of the house as well as the waves, we can find a radically new strategy of thought and project.

Eisenman has found a way of liberating architecture from Cartesian space and Euclidean form, overcoming this single interpretation of space and form. Namely, the possibility of 54-55 expressing a *space and form of transition*, where the compactness of form dissolves into spatial *vibration*.

The underlying problem is still that of opening or overcoming the finite dimension (of the project and of the body), and to a

54

To dislocate form from Cartesian rigidity, you can act through a deformation diagram, *namely the interaction of a typological or distributive scheme and the model of a* complex *natural phenomenon. The changing essence of the contemporary body, which is in perennial transition, corresponds to an architecture that is moving further away from the world of* objects *and drawing closer to that of* flows, *movements, connections.*

Peter Eisenman, model and, top of facing page, conceptual diagrams for the design of a library in Place des Nations, Geneva, 1997. Centre and bottom: Church for Rome 2000, *working models, model and ground plan, 1996.*

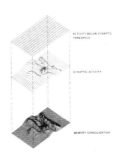

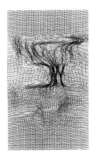

TWO-DIMENSIONAL REPRESENTATION
OF MEMORY CONSOLIDATION

VISCERAL NATURE

The exploration of the limit between formed and formless matter is translated into the articulation of enveloping or folded *cavities, capable of mediating organic and inorganic inspiration, natural and technological fascination.*

Natural examples of curved geometry and surfaces (taken from Charles Jencks, The Surface of Complexity; The Works of Frank O. Gehry*).*

From top to bottom, left to right: Frank Gehry, Lewis House, *Cleveland 1989-1995; Samsung Museum of Modern Art, South Korea, 1996;* Experience Music Project Museum, *1996; Chiat House, Telluride, Colorado, 1997; Berlin Conference Room, 1999.*

certain extent here again the operative strategy is the transition from a definite limit to a jagged margin. But the real discovery is that to dislocate form from Cartesian rigidity, you can act through a *deformation diagram*, i.e. a figurative architectural model (an expression of a traditional language) can interact with a *complex* natural phenomenon.

Leaving aside an interest in the technique itself, what must be emphasised is that the changing essence of the contemporary body, which is in perennial transition, corresponds to an architecture that increasingly tends to move away from the world of *objects* and draw closer to that of *flows*, movements, connections (as traced by diagrams).

While the interpretation of the biological processes of DNA guides the design for the Biocenter of Frankfurt University, in an even more strained way, the model of the undulating movement of waves produces a spatiality of dimensions, inclinations and constantly changing configurations in the house in Cadiz and later in the Arnoff Center in Cincinnati.

In the design for a church for Rome, the changing nature of *liquid crystal* serves as both metaphor and deformation diagram, strategy of thought, form and vision. A metaphor of transformation, the transitional state, the inter-being between formed and unformed matter, the deformation strategy of typological diagrams that sum up the functional requirements and contextual reality of the design. The profound structure of *hypersurfaces*, large screen walls that *open* the church to a connection with the world, creating a new bridge of continuity between real and virtual.

While the guiding metaphor and the conceptual diagram that transforms the functional layout in the design for a library in Geneva is the chaotic geometry of synaptic activity, the diagrams or traces of human memory, the memory of the ideal diagram of an earlier project for a house forms the basis for the project of the *Virtual House*. The complexity and lightness of the composition achieve extreme fluidity that binds the vagueness of thought and the vanishing lines of a form that, without a break, appears to pass from the finite to the potential, from the possible to the imaginary.

Greg Lynn, Stranded Sears Tower.

The body, as the place of life, *becomes in architecture a model for the constant activity of modification and adaptation through the exchange of information with the surrounding environment. In design the logic of forms and pre-formed, stable geometric figures is replaced by a logic based on the simulation of morphological processes that evolve over time through perturbations, upheavals, movements of contraction or expansion.*

John Frazer, Evolving virtual environment.

2.6 A Visceral Nature

Architecture as the search for a uterine dimension, the manifestation of a hidden nature, a living beginning that might suddenly wake up and emerge from its shell. Architecture as a confusion between interior and exterior, the construction of an outer space (external to the body) using the forms and principles of inner space (within the body). The exploration of the boundary between formed and formless matter.

The project for the Lewis house in Cleveland, jointly elaborated by Frank Gehry and Philip Johnson, shows us the surprising results of an architecture that has become a casing, pouch, spiral, shell, the horny covering of an unknown animal species. An architecture in which orthogonality is abandoned in favour of enveloping or *folded* cavities with a freedom of manipulating form that prompts the use of increasingly less canonical design strategies, culminating in the use of *drapery* to outline an environment that insinuates itself fluidly between the other elements. 57

The casing and the shell, flower buds, the fish-scale or snakeskin surface, the belly of the whale or the mountain, the movement or stratification of the earth's crust, but also the mechanical nature of binoculars, the coarse nature of asphalt and metallic mesh, the unprocessed nature of the waste produced by industrial civilisation, the heterogeneous and disharmonious nature of an industrial area as the project site for a new collective monument. Gehry's language collects, assembles and incorporates organic and inorganic inspiration, natural and technological fascination, plain aesthetics and sculptural sensitivity, simple volumes and contorted masses.

Above all, and in particular during the nineties, Gehry introjects landscape and moulds it like incandescent matter, crossed by a shudder that moves the volumes and surfaces into surprising informal configurations. Geographical rather than geometric shapes, because instead of measuring space they inscribe perturbations, upheavals, movements of contraction or expansion. In this way, the project forms part of the body's vital and dynamic nature, the circular and variable rhythm of breathing, the hidden but continuous activity of the bowels. A project whose genesis, by escaping the two-dimensional drawing of plans and sections, is above all three-dimensional and material (as shown by the material of the Lewis House), before becoming an electronic model of dynamic and interconnected information, an individualised design of the single element.

59 The central goal of Greg Lynn's research is the deconstruction of the architectural organism, in search of a fluid, flexible form that acquires corporeality and vitality as it becomes more *disorganic*. Freed from Euclidean rigidity, matter folds onto itself in search of those *lines of involution* that lead the organism in an opposite direction to that of the differentiation of species, namely the undifferentiated, the *common fact* (this expression was coined by Deleuze to whose writings Lynn explicitly and repeatedly refers) between the building and the ground, between architectural geometry and the orography of the site. While architectural form has still not been given an opportunity to mutate nor the capacity for transformation through which natural forms interact with the environment and its changeable nature, a first step towards liberating form from its immobility is possible through *topological deformation*. By this we mean the geometry of primary relations that allows a figure to be stretched, folded and distorted until it reaches its vanishing point, namely the point where it liquefies, dissolves and becomes non-figurative, where it cannot be assimilated to a predetermined type, before acquiring a new *informal* nature. An indispensable instrument, not only for the construction and control of these complex geometries but also their conception, is obviously a sophisticated electronic environment in which the *signs* are recognised as such and attributed a meaning that can be manipulated over time. By using computerised animation during the design phase, the *interaction* between the organism and the force flows that surround it can be visualised, guiding and soliciting adaptive responses or morphological deformations.

The idea of reproducing in the built-up environment the symbiotic behaviour and metabolic equilibrium typical of the natural environment is the guiding inspiration behind John
60 Frazer's research. The body, as the *place of life*, becomes a

model for the constant activity of modification and adaptation through the exchange of information with the surrounding environment. While in Lynn's case we can talk of an involutional paradigm, one that moves towards the original substance, the common fact of form and species, in Frazer's case the guiding idea is that of the institution of an evolutionary paradigm, broadly rooted in the world of biology and natural science.

Using computerised techniques, it is possible to replace the logic of forms and pre-formed geometric figures with a logic based on the simulation of morphological processes that, starting from an embryonic nucleus, evolve through the formation of the body. It is a question of developing the capacity for self-generation and self-organisation of forms in a process of multiple interaction with the information that characterises a given environment.

The virtuality of the design process would therefore enable a formal model to be developed totally unrelated to equilibrium, a fluctuating space between order and chaos. Real and virtual are indissoluble terms. One is the instrument of the other's thought. This allows it to master thought. No analogous form of architectural morphogenesis would be possible outside the electronic space.

2.7 Virtuality

But the life of forms in electronic space can take on even greater autonomy, pushing research into increasingly free ground, where autonomy of thought can produce new strategies to inhabit the world.

For Marcos Novak, this is the sense of being an architect, the essence of designing: working on the edges of the known world to "construct the frontiers of thought." This explains why the most radical architectural invention of the century for Novak is virtual space and the most critical theme of design is that of the threshold, the reciprocal hybridisation between real and virtual, between 3D space and space with x dimensions. Here the organ-less body becomes the space of a dilated dimension and temporality. And the further Novak

VIRTUALITY

The experience of a multidimensional spatiality is now possible in virtual space. Between this dilated dimensionality and real 3D space, the body becomes an inter-media surface, or the centre of a dual experience between real and virtual which acquires a new single dimension in the body itself.

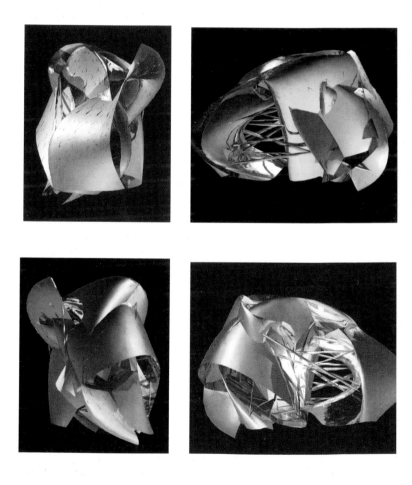

Marcos Novak, Data-driven form, *1998.*

explores the territories of virtual space, the more central the question of the body becomes: it acts as the threshold between two worlds, between the three dimensions of the bowels and the x dimensions of thought.

In fact, while the experience of spatial concepts revealed by 20th-century physics and mathematics is not possible in the real world, it is now possible in the virtual world (where it can be imagined and constructed, not as the replica of a 3D space, but as a multidimensional space).

In this way the body becomes an inter-media surface, the field for a dual experience between real space and virtual space which thereby acquires a new single dimension. And this dislocation of the corporeal experience can open the way to a new interrogation of the world and ourselves and, consequently, the possibility of imagining other possible *kinds of space*, other possible ways of being a body that-becomes-space.

2.8 Sensitivity

It is difficult to deny that through the possibilities offered by electronics, architecture tends to become a body, to become animated and develop that capacity for sensitivity, flexibility and interactivity that is the very essence of the living body.

Seen in this way, walls that are turned into *sensitive surfaces*, capable of acting as diaphragms to regulate the quantity of incoming light and *screen walls* transformed into luminous surfaces and signs, represent the first step in an attempt to transfer the body's sensorial, dynamic and communicative properties to the constructed environment.

But the transformation of the wall into a *hypersurface*, turning it from a physical boundary to space into a door onto the world of interconnections, is only the most evident aspect of a phenomenon that will revolutionise architecture well beyond its formal appearance.

The body as a model of self-organisation or the capacity to respond to change by producing change, points to the future of architecture, from *resistant* force to *active* force, capable of interacting with environmental and human solicitations. But above all, a technologically modified and modifiable body, linked to space by a new electromagnetic continuity tends to correspond to *corporeal* architecture, namely one capable of being aware of its own alterations (e.g. a state of structural strain), capable of contextual awareness (being aware of environmental alterations or the presence of a human being), as well as reacting by activating appropriate behaviours.

The awareness of the radical changes in the relationship between the body and space in the new electronic era and constant research into the meaning and opportunities offered by these changes is at the basis of the research carried out by the Media Laboratory of Massachusetts Institute of Technology directed by Nicholas Negroponte. In fact, although Negroponte founded the *Architecture Machine Group* in 1967 with the aim of reforming the process of architectural design through the "intimate association of two different species (man and machine)" (Negroponte 70), after several years work, the idea was overturned in the conviction that "architectural machines will not help us to design; instead, we will live inside them" (Negroponte 75). From the eighties onwards, after having founded Media Lab, research focused on the possibility of reciprocal connections between the body, architecture and information. The main intuition underlying Negroponte's research concerns the centrality of the man-machine interface or, more precisely, the problem of the transition from the *personal computer* to *personalised information* or informatisation (a passage that Negroponte defines as moving from the information era to the postinformation era). The transition from the mass to the individual, namely from depersonalised information (and computer), addressed to a generic user, to personalised information (and computer) tuned into specific interests and habits, will be achieved through the presence of *interface agents* ("bits that describe other bits") with the task of classifying and selecting information, or the task of creating a domain shared by a particular user and the machine.

This approach aimed at exalting personal individuality in relations with the machine (or *individualising* the machine to optimise its speech recognition capacity, for example) has prompted Media Lab to develop two potentially converging lines of research: the informatisation of the body and the informatisation of space.

While an *intelligent room* is an environment that is *sensitive* to human presence where, using TV cameras and microphones linked to a computer network, those present can use gestures and voice to communicate with the computer, as well as directly controlling *virtual environments* displayed on a wall screen, the *computer to be worn* is a sensitive garment that constantly supplies the user with information free from any spatial constraints (in the PAN system – Personal Area Network – bits at a maximum speed of one hundred thousand per second are transmitted through the body to connect, for example, a pair of rings acting as a loudspeaker and microphone to the telephone located in the shoe).

The next step consists of the connection between the body's "local network" and the network in a sensitive environment through interconnected electronic components. For example, "if your fridge notes that the milk is finished" by reading the bar codes on foodstuffs, it "can remind you to go and buy another pint on your way home." (Negroponte 95)

While the principle of enabling domestic appliances to communicate with each other and with the house owner may be regarded as a question of scarce architectural importance, the concept of the sensitisation of the environment aimed at specific personal needs (e.g. heat regulation determined on the basis of body temperature rather than that of the wall), forces us to reflect on the radical changes brought about by digital information in relations between the body and space.

A house that is sensitive to human presence, capable of following a person's movements through the various rooms and automatically controlling the opening and closing of doors, windows, lighting and heating was recently constructed in Sondrio, as part of the "Progetto Facile", in collaboration with Milan Polytechnic. It is a pilot apartment used to experiment with technological solutions that give persons with motor or cognitive disabilities, or the elderly the greatest degree of domestic autonomy, while maintaining a constant link with the nursing staff in a nearby hospital structure.

SENSITIVITY

If what distinguishes living from inorganic forms is essentially the capacity to exchange information *with the environment and, consequently, flexibility as the*

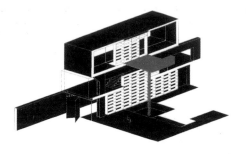

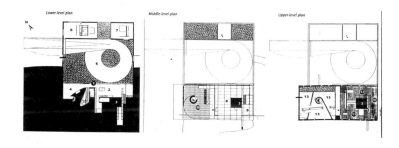

capacity to learn and modify, the key innovation of architecture in the second half of the 20th century is the aspiration to give buildings the sensitivity and flexibility of living systems.

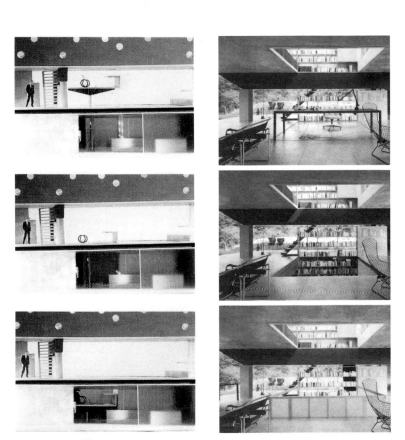

Rem Koolhaas, House in Bordeaux. Facing page, top to bottom: Diagram of moving floor, plans and longitudinal section. This page: left, section; right, view of intermediate level (with and without moving floor and with balustrade).

In addition to sensors for environmental security (smoke and water detectors) and occupancy sensors (to follow the occupant and facilitate movements by automatically turning on lighting, opening sliding doors, operating electric appliances and, if necessary, detecting and reporting the user's difficulties or immobility), a fundamental role is played by a portable voice recognition instrument installed on the wheelchair and at the head of the bed. Other functions provided by the control software concern the processing of information linked to specific rehabilitation programmes, the management of the house (at different times of day) and, for those with cognitive disabilities, visitor recognition.

A very different concept, but one that stems from a similar desire to increase the awareness of space, seen no longer as a barrier but as an extension, a prosthesis or *vehicle* to add movement to the body, has inspired the project by Nox **72-73** Architects: *FreshH$_2$0eXPO*. The central idea of the project is to emerge the body in an underwater experience (the experience of the liquidity of water, but above all the experience of the body surrounded by moving matter), working on the principle of the wheelchair, a skateboard, rollerblades or the wheel in general, namely the concept of a motor geometry or a prosthetic mobility provided by an object-carrier (in this instance, the pavilion itself) which becomes part of the action. The idea is based on the logic that attributes (or recognises) the body's natural tendency to *incorporate* anything that might be useful to integrate or extend its own motor system. A classic example (mentioned by Spuybroek in the presentation of the project) is the driver and the car. The possibility of carrying out perfect manoeuvres in extremely tight spaces can only be explained by the driver's ability to *feel* the car's manoeuvring space, in other words, the car becomes the driver's second skin.

The example of the imaginary limb is even more convincing: the missing foot that hurts when it is not there, and stops hurting when the artificial limb is fitted. The possibility of walking restores the body's *motor integrity* and this is totally predominant over the foot's organic or mechanical nature.

But perhaps the most surprising example of the body's constant tendency to see itself as part of its surroundings, its complete integration in a single system of movement is the perception that a nomad has of space (judged by us as *outdoors*). In fact, with the same degree of naturalness that the mechanical foot and car are seen as part of the body, the nomad incorporates the whole of space under his own skin, because his tent is a house that never interrupts his progress, but on the contrary accompanies it: space is an extension, a prosthesis or vehicle for his own movement.

This logic of continuity or the body seen as part of the world overturns perspective and Euclidean logic and turns it inside out, upside down in a system of circular or gravitational orientation centred on the body. It is the logic underlying the spatial layout of the Fresh Water Pavilion.

Using a geometry in which the ground is all around us, a volume in which it is impossible to distinguish the ceiling from the floor, the vertical from the horizontal, architecture accelerates the movement of the body, involving it or precipitating it in an interactive game that (through a system of sensors and actuators) mixes hardware and software, constructive and informative material, resistant and liquid matter, images, lights, sounds and colours. The pavilion becomes a system of real and virtual waves, provocatively sensitive to human presence and fitted with their own biorhythm, influenced by the weather conditions and the water level outside the pavilion.

The body's journey through architecture is transformed into a journey inside a corporeal architecture, in a damp electronic and underwater belly where inert and living matter look for a new meeting point and continuity.

3. The Logic of Complexity

3.1 Electronic Space

The embryo outside its mother's body, the astronaut, or man outside the earth walking in space and the cybernaut, man outside reality on a virtual journey, are three emblematic figures of a phenomenon of the *dislocation* of the body, rooted in the

72

The body as a model of self-organisation or capacity to respond to change by producing change, points to the future of architecture, from resistant force to active force. A system capable being aware of its own alterations, capable of contextual awareness and interacting with these stresses by acti-

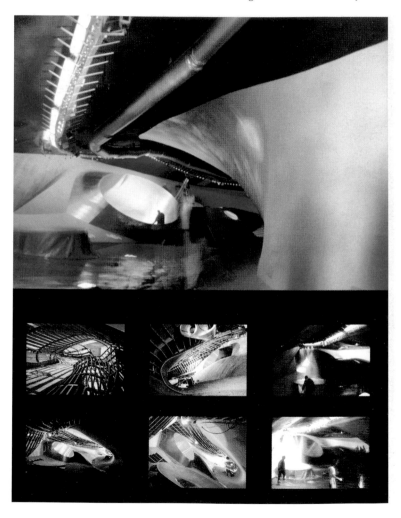

Nox Architects, Fresh Water Pavilion, *Holland, 1997.*

vating appropriate behaviours. *In this sense, the transformation of a wall into a* hypersurface, *from a physical boundary to space into a door onto the world of interconnections is only the most evident aspect of a phenomenon that will revolutionise architecture well beyond its formal appearance.*

Nox Architects, Fresh Water Pavilion, *Holland, 1997.*

broader process of the *deterritorialisation* of society. In fact, the further man develops his technical capacities, the further he extends his own domain, leaving behind his place of birth. In this sense history appears to be a gradual process of moving away or uprooting, conquering increasingly distant points of view and acquiring greater margins of action. In the same way that the ancient world was characterised by the conquest of the mainland and the modern world by the crossing of the oceans, our contemporary horizon is defined by possession of the skies and cosmic space. Access to a new virtual dimension appears to crown this progress of gradual emancipation from the materiality of earth and our birthplace, clearly emphasising that we are conquering much more than mere *distance*.

"The alliance between technique and air" (Boatto 92) and the dimensional leap that this permits, has produced a radical change in the forms of life on earth, rather than an emancipation from earth. More precisely, electronics, the aerial technique, has revolutionised man's entire range of possibilities, in other words, his way of continuing to be essentially *terrestrial*. As McLuhan writes:

> Electric lighting gave the cultural complex of man's extensions in the home and in the city an organic flexibility that was unknown to any other age [...]. Lighting as the extension of our possibilities offers the clearest example of how these extensions can modify our perception [...] the medium is the message, and when the light is on there is a world of senses that disappears as soon as the light is switched off. (McLuhan 97)

The *organic flexibility* provided by light is the revolution that distinguishes this age from every other.

Electronics has transformed the world into a total field of interdependent events open to social participation, making each of us immediately *present* at everything that happens, and *accessible* from any point in space. To this extent, while it is true that "all media are active metaphors with the power of translating experience into new forms", the most powerful translation that electronics allows is not that of a virtual body, but rather that our real body is immersed in this total world of experience, a world where we can acquire (mediated) experience of both outside and inside our bodies, of every part of the world and universe, the infinitely large and the infinitely small, the infinitely immense times and spaces of the stars, and the infinitely minute spaces of atoms.

What is even more extraordinary is that the flexibility of electronics has allowed us to reveal the extreme flexibility of a natural world that is very different from the mechanical world, governed by exact mathematical laws formulated by the first scientific revolution. During the course of the 20th century, but above all from the sixties onwards, thanks to the use of increasingly efficient computers, the conceptual scheme of modern science elaborated by Galileo and Descartes and completed by Newton, finally hit a crisis.

The concept of nature as an objective and causal order, governed by laws that regulate phenomena in a deterministic manner, making them foreseeable, and the concept of science as mathematical knowledge based on calculation and quantitative measurement, was found to be on the verge of contradiction when related to the chaotic, creative and unforeseeable nature of living systems. The quantitative approach was inadequate to study and describe phenomena whose complexity could only be understood using visual and qualitative measurement. The *electronic machine*, as opposed to the *perspective machine*, played an undeniable role as the instrument of the conceptual revolution that characterises the new scientific IT revolution.

The computer countered the objective, mathematical and measuring approach of perspective by its capacity to look at chaos and discover the new patterns of *order* characterised by their open and dynamic nature, sensitive to the surrounding world and influenced by them in unforeseen ways.

While the rigid and metric logic of perspective allowed the profundity of the world to be reduced to a single plane through a strategy of boundless power to lead the multitude of points to a single vanishing point, and the variety of elements to a single scale of comparison, the *liquid* nature of digital information now allows us to dialogue with the most secret and vital aspects of nature. In other words, by leaving the traditional narrow paths of thought and Cartesian and Euclidean representation, we can access the jagged measurement of clouds and mountains, the *dynamic, flexible and sensitive* nature of the body as a living system.

3.2 The Corporeal Machine

The question of *sensitivity* now indissolubly links the body, machines and architecture.

If the distinguishing factor between living and inorganic forms is essentially the capacity to *exchange information* with the environment and, consequently, flexibility in terms of the capacity to learn and modify, the key innovation of architecture in the second half of the 20th century, characterised by its growing intimacy with machines, is the aspiration to give buildings the sensitivity and flexibility of living systems. Whereas during the early 20th century, the conquest of *transparency* became the symbol of a profoundly renewed construction world, the conquest of *interactivity*, namely the possibility of active relations between the building and the variable forces surrounding it, appears to be the leading edge of a radical new renewal (as affirmed on several occasions in this series).

But, although the key to this renewal is generally thought to be the possible integration between architecture and electronic components, the difficulties of the machine in tackling and resolving *spatial and corporeal* problems prompt us to look further and to recall that the frontier of a new sensitivity calls above all for a radical transformation of the machine. This transformation in turn calls for a genuine inversion of the terms of the problem: to make space *intelligent* to the electronic system, we must make the machine corporeal, or in other words give it spatial intelligence. It is necessary to design new *types of machine* that can replace the classic analytical and linguistic logic with a visual, spatial and metaphorical *logic of the senses*.

Whereas the *logical rigour* that was reckoned to be the most complex human function to attribute to a machine was achieved relatively easily within the space of a few decades, the *common sense* typical of children in infancy, which underlies our awareness of space and context, has presented programming problems that are still unresolved.

A machine can therefore resolve extremely complex algorithms with no problem, but if asked to identify the occupants of a room, follow their movements and interpret their gestures, expression or voices, or to change a wall from a *barrier* into a *medium* of information chosen and assembled from the environment, the machine fails.

The fact is that although an extremely important transition has occurred from Pascal's calculator to the machines that we now refer to as *expert systems*, namely systems capable of carrying out functions other than pure calculus in very specific sectors for which they have been programmed, this evolution has resulted in a marked specialisation. Moreover, this specialisation is substantially an alternative to the propensity towards *flexibility* typical of the intelligence of living systems. The task of creating an integrated platform (namely one that is able to manage different sources of information and knowledge simultaneously), capable of elementary behaviour like recognising an object on the basis of visual information (the basic level of *perceptive categorisation*), is an essential stage prior to the definitive transition from a computer to a machine capable of interacting with persons and the physical world, and consequently becoming the core of a flexible and interactive architecture.

Although a preliminary and conceptually simple improvement in quality can be achieved by moving from a blind and deaf machine, connected to the world only by a keyboard and a mouse, to a machine that can see and hear what we do, the decision to equip the classic computer with a system of sensors is in practice not of great help in the search for a *sensitive machine*. It is not enough to add sensorial organs to a machine whose structure is conceived as rigid architecture, able to process (sequentially) only what it was programmed to perform, to make it interact with the extreme variability of the physical world, a world full of nuances, shadows and murmurs that mask the main information. In order to achieve this inter-action, the machine must *become a body*, it must be able to *take stock*. In other words, it must change radically by master-ing that logic of the senses which we call the *logic of the body*.

It is a question of redesigning the machine not as a metaphor of a mind split in dualistic terms from its body, but as the metaphor of a mind that is even more incarnated through the body and deeply characterised by its existence in space. This means replacing the analytical and deductive logic that gov-erns processing with a global and associative strategy.

3.3 The Architecture of the Machine

In order to grasp the concrete meaning of these two alterna-tives, we should return to an analysis of the architecture of the machine as it was traditionally conceived and as we try to think of it today.

> Von Neuman's sequential architecture computer, whose concept underlies the whole of computing, consists of two essential parts: a central processing unit (CPU) and a passive memory for data. The system works when the CPU executes, one after the other, a sequence of instructions on data filed in the memory. These instructions form part of the programme that someone has written and entered into the machine, without it having the possibility of altering or amending it. (Fornero 1996)

The fact that this structure has enabled the machine to carry out a number of operations peculiar to human intelligence (operations requiring exceptional logical rigour, like computa-tion, which other living beings are unable to use) has prompt-ed the conviction that the simulation of intelligence as a whole could be realised, irrespective of the physical neurological structure that is the backup for intelligence in living beings. In fact, if we compare the computer architecture described above with what little we know of the brain's architecture, it is diffi-cult to find effective analogies. Our head does not appear to contain anything that resembles a programme or central instruction unit, far less a "passive archive of data". It is equally difficult to "identify a single sequence of activities while all the rest remains inactive, and it is difficult to conceive a brain that remains unchanged over time, and does not learn."

Based on these considerations, starting from the incapacity of the traditional machine to tackle problems relating to the extremely chaotic and unforeseeable nature of the physical world, rather than an abstract mathematical domain (problems that call for a high level of flexibility and a capacity to adapt to the infinite variety of situations and possible nuances), and proceeding to re-examine the model of an *abstract* machine which is programmatically different to the structural principles of living beings (characterised by an open, adaptive and evolutionary architecture), an attempt was made to artificially emulate the *physical basis* for the principles of life and intelligence (using an approach known as *connectionist*).

Emulating the structural and functional principles of the brain is the strategy used by neural networks when constructing a machine that aims to replace the programming, sequential and aseptic approach used by the traditional computer with the learning capacity, awareness of context, flexibility of function and other capacities typical of living beings.

> The brain is made up of several subsystems that work in parallel and its architecture comprises a large number of relatively simple units (neurons) linked together by synaptic connections which transmit activation and inhibition and constantly alter their conductivity in the light of experience. The neural networks are distributed systems with a high degree of parallelism. (Fornero 96)

Systems where all the units not only operate in parallel, but where there is no CPU to coordinate the mechanisms. Where there is no functional determinism typical of traditional computers because, on the contrary, networks learn by modifying themselves through experience, regulating the parameters known as synaptic weights (by analogy with the synapses that link the neurons in the brain) to allow "the performance most suited for the execution of particular tasks."

Towards a postorganic architecture

Our horizon is characterised by a paradigmatic reversal of perspective. While the body, invaded and dilated by technology becomes architecture, architecture in turn looks to the body, not as a model of order and formal measurement, but as a model of sensitivity, flexibility, intelligence and communicative capacity. Whereas the body designs its own spatial extension, architecture designs its corporeal future. If the revolution brought about by

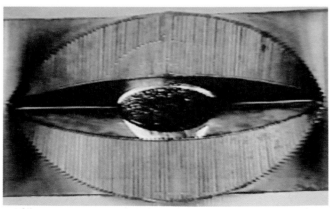

Top: Santiago Calatrava, Planetarium, Science City, Valencia, Spain, 1991-2000. Bottom and facing page: Santiago Calatrava, Winking Eye, *1985.*

electronics led, in our opinion, to the inclusion of a new organic flexibility in the complex of man's life and activities, we have now perhaps gone one step further. It is hard not to believe that the biotechnological revolution will open the doors to a hybrid territory, an intermediate dimension between real and virtual, a matter halfway between organic and inorganic, a code of information that blends the genetic and digital.

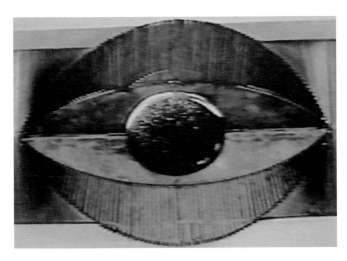

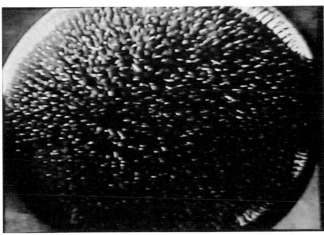

The active role of the memory is essential here. Training the network calls for a series of examples and the relative responses, since this is how the network learns – by modifying and altering the weights of the connections.

The traditional logical and linguistic concept of learning is replaced by an associative mnemonic process, whose profound visual and spatial roots can be illustrated in a simple practical example. How can we make a machine move in real space, in other words how can it be made capable of self-piloting its movements?

The classic system entails an extremely complex procedure of calculation based on the precise definition of the route, for example, by determining the distance from walls and any other obstacles. In this case, either the machine has previously memorised the map of the space through which it moves (making it difficult to tackle unknown conditions or avoid unexpected obstacles, like a piece of furniture out of place or a passing person), or the ability to detect space and its own position within it, as well as calculating the route, becomes an incredibly complex task.

One possible alternative is that the machine should learn to follow the midline of a corridor, for example, associating every TV image (which is elaborated by extracting the corners) with an appropriate direction command. The image obtained is then compared with those memorised during training and the one that most closely resembles it is extracted, sending the actuators the navigation commands associated with it. For example, if the image detects the closeness of the right wall, the associated command will require a shift to the left.

Using this system of *proceeding by images*, the machine can navigate itself through unknown settings.

The quantitative measurement is replaced by a qualitative measurement. The calculation process is replaced by a metaphorical process. In this way, the unknown structure of the corridor is transferred into a known spatial structure. This capacity to translate experience permits considerable *flexibility* of movement through space.

Of course, this does not mean that the neural network can

satisfy and attain the research horizons of a new sensitive machine. On the contrary, in many ways it emphasises the extreme difficulties and uncertainties involved in this approach.

But it is certainly an approach that revolutionises earlier research and the key to this revolution is having overcome the *mechanicalism* through a new convergence between organic logic and mechanical logic, between the life of the body and the life of forms. A convergence that overturns the dialectics of alterity that characterised the modern age, in favour of a new transversality, a new form of dialogue and meeting between objects, indefinite measurement and flexible forms, a hazy boundary that permits and encourages wide margins of leeway and overlap.

If the revolution brought about by electronics led to the inclusion of a new organic flexibility in the complex of man's life and activities, we have now perhaps gone one step further.

After the transition from mechanics to electronics, a new transformation invests the machine and carries it into the field of biology. What is the message or revolution of the *biotechnological era*? After the earth, the sea, the sky and the virtual, what will be the new dimensional leap implicit in this new alliance between technology and life? What new territory will extend the horizons and man's field of action?

It is hard not to believe that the current revolution will open the doors to a hybrid territory, an intermediate dimension between real and virtual, a matter halfway between organic and inorganic, a code of information that blends the genetic and digital. This is the postorganic horizon that the key of the body has pointed us towards as the far-reaching convergence between the living landscape of the body and the built-up landscape of architecture.

While the finite and absolute measurement of the body's surface was both the centre of a harmonious universe and a guarantee for the objective nature of beauty and thought, today the chaotic, jagged and mysterious forms of the body's visceral nature lay the foundations for a new measure of complexity.

Further Reading

Towards a Postorganic Paradigm

In 1996 Teresa Macrì published *Il corpo postorganico. Sconfinamento della performance*. The book opens with a quotation from Mario Perniola's *Il sex-appeal dell'inorganico*, a book that in turn opens by tracing the origin of this expression (and a critical reflection on the new alliance between *objects and the senses* or between "the way of being of an object and human sensitivity") to Walter Benjamin and his work *Paris, 19th century capital. The "passages" of Paris*. Macrì writes: "The body in construction is a fantastic hybridisation between organic and inorganic, between particle matter and silicon chips. […] a technological corporealisation and a technologised corporealisation." Outlining the horizon of a radical change in aesthetic and cultural sensitivity ("Having exhausted the great historical task of comparing ourselves to God and animals, which dates back in the West to the time of the Greeks, the object has now become the focus for our attention"), Perniola writes à propos of Libeskind and Hadid: "In both their works architecture becomes the design of a world in which all distinctions have been abolished between technical object and living body […] Architecture is no longer a metaphor of the human body, using an organicistic model, because the body is itself architecture, even its innermost and most secret parts: for example, an intestinal endoscopy offers direct imaging of one's own abdomen. It offers a plastic landscape which I can see through technology."

The question of this new extreme possibility of imaging and manipulating the body has prompted a lively debate over the past few years which crosses all subject fields, representing the tip of the debate on the *virtualisation* of society. Catastrophists and enthusiasts fear or encourage an inevitable *expropriation of thought* (the loss of alterity between subject and object, man and machine, and man's consequent reduction to a remote-controlled automaton), or an exciting *escape into thought* (the realisation of a "society of the mind" of subjects freed from physical and corporeal constraints). If we take stock on the basis of these extreme prospects, it is worth recalling first of all that a revolution is certainly underway and, whether we like it or not, in the same way as the computer has entered architectural design, it has also entered our homes, our lives, our bodies. This is not a *neutral* tool, but one that transforms design, life and *reality*. A second aspect worth emphasising is the concept of reality, and in particular, the concept of *authenticity*, especially concerning the *nature* of the body. If it is true that media transform us, providing an extension of our capacities and the possibility of transforming our self-perception and our perception of the world, and if this process of *extending* the capacity of thought and action has constituted the essence of man and the history of humanity right from the outset, how should we define *authentic* man, or how can we define *man* if we deprive him of his ambition to conquer the moon? Is a man walking in space (or with a *pacemaker*) perhaps less genuine than any other man walking on earth? Once again, fear or our control syndrome (man reduced to an automaton) hides the nostalgic desire for a single body, a unity, *one* meaning, *one* reason, one certainty. In a work that describes contemporary society from a very different point of view compared to the previously cited authors, Ian Chambers writes: "Despite Baudrillard's constant attempt to place himself 'beyond' [...] in his description of the computer he still reveals his faith in one original, in a state of affairs that existed before their representation, reproduction, simulation [...] There is no a priori, no thought without a means of expression, mediation, scene, performance." (Chambers 96)

The following works provide a *transversal* bibliography on the intermingling between the architectural body and the IT revolution in the contemporary age.

Deleuze 80 - Gilles Deleuze, Félix Guattari, *Thousand Plateaus: Capitalism and Schizophrenia*, Minnesota Press, Minneapolis 1987.

Brand 93 - Stewart Brand, *Media Lab: Inventing the Future at MIT*, Penguin Books, New York 1989.

Vidler 93 - Anthony Vidler, *The Architectural Uncanny*, MIT Press, Cambridge, Mass. 1993.

Ferraro 94 - Angela Ferraro, Gabriele Montagano (eds.), *La scena immateriale. Linguaggi elettronici e mondi virtuali*, Costa & Nolan, Genova 1994.

Perniola 94 - Mario Perniola, *Il sex appeal dell'inorganico*, Einaudi, Torino 1994.

Haraway 95 - Donna Haraway, *Simians, Cyborgs and Women: the Reinvention of Nature*, Routledge, New York 1991.

Caronia 96 - Antonio Caronia, *Il corpo virtuale. Dal corpo robottizzato al corpo disseminato nelle reti*, Muzio, Padova 1996.

Chambers 96 - Ian Chambers, *Paesaggi migratori. Cultura e identità nell'epoca postcoloniale*, Costa & Nolan, Genova 1996.

De Kerckhove 96 - Derrick de Kerckhove, *The Skin of Culture*, Somerville Press, Toronto 1996.

Macrì 96 - Teresa Macrì, *Il corpo postorganico. Sconfinamenti della performance*, Costa & Nolan, Genova 1996.

Capra 97 - Fritjof Capra, *The Web of Life: A New Scientific Understanding of Living Systems*, Anchor Books, New York 1997.

Davidson 97 - Cynthia Davidson (ed.), *ANYBODY*, MIT Press, Cambridge 1997.

McLuhan 97 - Marshall McLuhan, *Understanding Media: the Extension of Man*, MIT Press, Cambridge, Mass. 1994.

Prestinenza 98 - Luigi Prestinenza Puglisi, *Hyperarchitecture. Spaces in the Electronic Age*, Birkhäuser, Basel 1999 (Italian edition: *Spazi nell'età dell'elettronica*, Testo & Immagine, Torino 1998).

1. The Dismeasurable Body

1.1 The Man in the Circle

The objectivity of the body becomes an essential launching pad for the objectivity of sight through the *visual machine* that, for the first time, measures sight, attributing a new cognitive value to representation, a principle of authenticity. A century before Galileo's assault on the heavens and the scientific reflections of Cartesian thought, the theory of perspective set out in the works by Alberti and Brunelleschi, and later by Leonardo and the Renaissance treatises in general, raised the *problem of method*, the problem of an objective, quantitative and universal approach to reality. On perspective: Erwin Panofsky, *Perspective as Symbolic Form*, Zone Books, New York 1991. On aesthetics and Renaissance architecture: Rudolf Wittkower, *Architectural Principles in the Age of Humanism*, Academy Editions, Chichester 1998. On the new "scientific awareness" of the Renaissance: Dino Formaggio, *L'arte. Come idea e come esperienza*, Mondadori, Milano 1990. For an introduction to the problem of "the value of knowledge" in modern philosophy, Emanuele Severino, *La filosofia moderna*, Rizzoli, Milano 1984.

1.2 The Eyes of Olympia

While the transition from a theocentric vision of the world to an anthropocentric vision raised the urgent question of the truth and foundations of knowledge, prompting a series of *safety measures* to exclude arbitrariness or madness, the reconquest of a multiplicity of viewpoints coincided in the 16th and 17th century with the final disintegration of the harmonious Renaissance universe. Exploration and colonisation, the division of the Church and the Copernican revolution prompted a totally new vision of the world. The visual machine was turned into a *stage machine*, an instrument of the marvellous and the possible, *trompe-l'oeil*, and later camera optica and diorama: systems of representation in which the realism of the image was pushed as far as the hyperreality of illusion. The next step saw the machine passing from optical instrument to artifice, the subject of *artificial sight*. Hoffman's tale is emblematic in this sense. In the tale, the young Nathaniel (the biblical name given to one of Christ's disciples who, because of his *readiness to see*, was promised that he would see much greater things) falls in love with Olympia, glimpsing her first behind a tent and then spying on her through a telescope. But although the young man comes close to the automaton and falls in love with her through the *mediation* of an optical instrument, it is the desire for *relationship* that brings Olympia's eyes to life, making them bleed when they were thrown at Nathaniel during a fight between the constructors of the female automaton. Between the 18th and 20th century, in literature and cinema artificial sight became the symbol of a universe marked by radical transformations, which were both fascinating and terrifying. From *Metropolis* to *Blade Runner*, the artificial insinuated itself into the collective imagination as a subtle invasion, a replicant that was increasingly difficult to distinguish from humans. On the transformation of the perspective machine into a stage machine: Giulio Carlo Argan, *Immagine e persuasione. Saggi sul barocco*, Feltrinelli, Milano 1986; Renzo Dubbini, *Geografie dello sguardo. Visione e paesaggio in età moderna*, Einaudi, Torino 1994. On the body and artificial sight, in addition to Caronia 96: Franco Speroni, *Sotto il nostro sguardo*, Costa & Nolan, Genova 1995. On the aesthetics of *Einfuhlung*: Renato De Fusco, *L'idea di architettura. Storia della critica da Viollet-le-Duc a Persico*, Etas Libri, Milano 1989. On the re-elaboration of "ego" and the birth of "psychological" man: Carl E. Schorske, *Fin-de-siècle Vienna: Politics and Culture*, Vintage Books, New York 1981.

1.3 Space with Figures

The reflection on the body in the new mechanical universe prompted the formulation of new theories of movement during the early decades of the 20th century. These included biomechanics, elaborated by the Russian producer Vsevolod Mejerchol'd, a preparatory technique for theatrical action based on a sequence of exercises aimed at the discovery and study of the mechanics of natural movement. Mejerchol'd's research is closely linked to constructivism, in the shared aspiration to a social and artistic renewal incarnated through the affirmation of a new mechanical universe. On the theatre in Bauhaus: O. Schlemmer, L. Moholy-Nagy, F. Molnàr, *Theater of the Bauhaus*, John Hopkins University Press, Baltimore 1996; RoseLee Goldberg, *Performance Art. From Futurism to the Present*, Harry N. Abrams, London 1996. On biomechanics and the theatrical avantgarde: Eugenio Barba, *La canoa di carta*, Il Mulino, Bologna 1993. The expression "prosthetic architecture" is taken from *Absent Bodies* by Ignasi de Sola-Morales and the concept of "therapeutic architecture" from *The Medical Body in Modern Architecture* by Beatriz Colomina, both in Davidson 97.

1.4 The Cyborg

During the 20th century, art, literature and philosophy, psychoanalysis and science have radically questioned the *dimensions* of corporeality. Against this background, one of the thoughts about the body that has had major repercussions on contemporary architecture stems from French philosophy which, by emphasising the "obsession with sight, spatiality, corporeality that represented one of the aspects of Husserlian phenomenology" (Bodei 97), took the destructuring of the classic subject as the centre or root of its own reasoning. After Foucault, with Derrida and Deleuze, the crisis of subject and reason opened the way to a way of thought aimed at deconstructing the univocal nature of sense and form, the being and *logos*. The purpose was to give a voice to the margins: the secrets or silences of a text, breaking down the reasoned, rational and apparently certain meaning to discover in that *différance* a truth that escaped the univocal nature of reason (Derrida). To rediscover *the intensive nature of the body*: a *cosmic and molecular* feeling that links bodies and animals, objects, stones and machines together in a single chain, a single *folded* space, a single hybrid and transversal Nature, drawing *a line of involution where form does not cease to be dissolved* (Deleuze). Very different but equally important in the current debate on the body is the thought of another two French intellectuals. Paul Virilio, a town-planner and expert on technosciences (one of the most attentive critics, not to say prophets, of technological catastrophism), defines the body as *the last urban territory*: "How can we not understand the extent to which these radiotechniques [...] may in the future start to overturn not only the nature of the human environment, his territorial body but, above all, that of the individual and his animal body after the exploitation of the territory through heavy material infrastructures (roads, railways) gives way to control of the intangible environment (satellites, fibre optic cables) attached to the *terminal human body*, this interactive being which is both transmitter and receiver." (Virilio 97) Equally significant are the words of Jean Baudrillard: "Am I a man, am I a machine? There is no answer to this anthropological question [...] There was no ambiguity in the relations between the worker and the traditional machine. The worker was always in some way extraneous to the machine, and therefore alienated from it. He preserved his precious quality of alienated man. On the contrary, the new technologies, the new machines, the new images, the interactive screens do not alienate me at all. They include me in an *integrated circuit*." (Baudrillard 94) For a discussion of the body in contemporary art and society: Jean Baudrillard, *Lo Xerox e l'infinito*, in Ferraro 94; Stelarc, da *Strategie psicologiche a cyberstrategie*, in Pier Luigi Capucci (ed.), *Il corpo tecnologico*, Baskerville, Bologna 1994; Jean-Luc Nancy, *Corpus*, Cronopio, Napoli 1995; Francesca Alfano Miglietti, *Identità mutanti*, Costa & Nolan, Genova 1997; Paul Virilio, *Vitesse de libération*, Galilée, Paris 1995; Pierre Lévy, *Becoming Virtual*, Plenum Trade, New York 1998. For an introduction to contemporary philosophy: Remo Bodei, *La filosofia del Novecento*, Donzelli, Roma 1997. In addition to Deleuze 80, by Gilles Deleuze, *Francis Bacon: logique de la sensation*, Editions de la Différance, Paris 1981; by Jacques Derrida, *Margins of Philosophy*, University of Chicago Press, Chicago 1997, and *Sproni: gli stili di Nietzsche*, Feltrinelli, Milano 1991.

2. THE PROJECT OF CHAOS

2.1 Utopia and Chaotic Attractors
On radical avantgarde research and its relations with current architectural research: Luigi Prestinenza Puglisi, *This is Tomorrow*, Testo & Immagine, Torino 1999, series ControSegni, n. 5. The concept of *attractor* developed by the mathematics of complexity to study chaotic phenomena is used here for two important reasons. The first is that while an important mathematical intuition to bring order to chaos was to shift the attention from analytical logic to visual patterns, an analogous step from the classic logic of the *formal* correspondence between body and architecture to a logic of complexity that relates the organisational principles of the body and architecture, is the central intuition that gives a new corporeal matrix to the dynamics of design. Moreover, the concept of attractor helps us to recall that *chaotic behaviour* in the scientific sense is very different from casual or completely irregular behaviour which responds to the patterns shown by *complex dynamic problems*. On the mathematics of complexity and the theory of chaos, see Capra 97. On the relation between architectural body and IT revolution, in addition to the aforesaid Davidson 97: Elizabeth Diller, Ricardo Scofidio, *Flesh: Architectural Probes*, Princeton, New York 1994; Christian Thomsen, *Sensuous Architecture. The Art of Erotic Building*, Prestel, New York 1998; and the following issues of *Architectural Design*: *Modern Pluralism*, n. 95, 1992; *Organic Architecture*, n. 106, 1993; *Folding in Architecture*, n. 102, 1993; *Architects in Cyberspace*, n. 118, 1995; *Integrating Architecture*, n. 123, 1996; *After Geometry*, n. 127, 1997; *Hypersurface Architecture*, n. 133, 1998; *Architects in Cyberspace II*, n. 136, 1998.

2.2 Urban Dismeasurement
The fundamental characteristic of Stalker's research into the complex and chaotic nature of the modern city is the predominance of *action* over *representation*, name-

ly the use of the body as an instrument of perceptive inquiry into space, crossing the territory by foot and visiting it at different times of day and night as a strategy to enter and become part of the dynamics of the place. From this point of view, *current territories* form a single urban space where the experience or *adventure* that the city has cancelled is still possible: the experience of body to body with space, the body surrounded, immersed in untamed space, where anything might happen, anyone could be seen or met. Where crossing the city becomes a creative act, the outline of a subjective geography, a map between the numerous possibilities, a spatiality constructed within the itinerary. By Stalker, *Stazioni. Paesaggi e passaggi nei territori del transito*, in Massimo Ilardi e Paolo Desideri (eds.), *Attraversamenti. I nuovi territori dello spazio pubblico*, Costa & Nolan, Genova 1997; Lorenzo Romito, *Stalker*, in P. Lang (ed.), *Suburban Discipline*, Princeton, New York 1997. On Land Art and on a panorama of artistic research from the sixties to the nineties: Lea Vergine, *L'arte in trincea*, Skira Editore, Milano 1996. On the movements that formed part of the "Situationist International": Mirella Bandini, *L'estetico, il politico*, Officina, Roma 1977. By Guy Debord, *The Society of the Spectacle*, Zone Books, New York 1994. On the new meaning of the boundary within the city as "a setting for differences" and on the perceptive relationship between body and space: Franco La Cecla, *Città creola di fine millennio*, in *La città è nuda*, Edizioni Volontà, Milano 1995; *Perdersi. L'uomo senza ambiente*, Laterza, Roma-Bari 1988.

2.3 Architectural Dismeasurement

In *Six Conversations* (Academy Editions, London 1993), Cook writes: "In the sixties there was a radical distinction between the hardware – the design of spaces and buildings – and the software – the effect of information and programming on the environment. […] I have sometimes described my recent work as 'melted architecture'. This definition is linked to the search for a perpetual state of transition […]. A state of disintegration or synthesis of the elements."

When presenting the project for the Carnuuntum Museum (*Hic Saxa Loquuntur*, exhibition catalogue, Berlin 1995), Hadid and Schumacher write: "We used different elements of the structure of geological formations (stratifications, cave-ins) as models, as well as human interventions in the landscape, above all quarries (cavities, terraces). The four single projects were seen as the first fragments of a new culture […]. This project [the amphitheatre] expresses the basic theme of architecture as an extension of the landscape in the sense of a flat landscape from natural to artificial". See also: Cesare De Sessa, *Zaha Hadid. Eleganze dissonanti*, Testo & Immagine, Torino 1996. By Lebbeus Woods, *Anarchitecture. Architecture is a Political Art*, Academy Editions, London 1992. By Daniel Libeskind, *Radix-Matrix*, Prestel, New York 1997.

2.4 Uprooting

On the progressive uprooting of contemporary society: Marc Augé, *Non-places: Introduction to an Anthropology of Supermodernity*, Verso, London-New York 1995; P. Desideri e M. Ilardi, *op. cit.*; William Mitchell, *City of Bits*, MIT Press,

Boston 1996. The words of Ito are clear and significant (*El Croquis*, no.71, 1995): "Although they are not visible to sight, our bodies are constantly exposed to the air of technology, they respond to it and our biological rhythms are synchronised with it [...] When we use a filter to screen the air crossed by invisible information, the information becomes visible. Architecture today should become a filter of this kind used to display information [...]. Whereas the ideal life of the electric age was embodied in the space of modern living, we have not yet found an ideal space for life in the information age".

2.5 Fluidity

In *Visions Unfolding: Architecture in the Age of Electronic Media* (recently republished in Galofaro 99), Eisenman writes: "During the fifty years since the Second World War, a paradigm shift has taken place that should have profoundly affected architecture: this was the shift from the mechanical paradigm to the electronic one. [...] Suppose for a moment that architecture could be conceptualised as a Moebius strip, with an unbroken continuity between interior and exterior. What would this mean for vision? Gilles Deleuze has proposed just such a possible continuity with his idea of the fold. For Deleuze, folded space articulates a new relationship between vertical and horizontal, figure and ground, inside and out [...]. The fold presents the possibility of an alternative to the gradual space of the Cartesian order." Highlighting how the technique he calls blurring enables the organisation of a new way of designing, creating metaphorical or real relations with the context, on the subject of the Guardiola House Antonino Saggio writes: "The waves on the beach over which the house looks are not an object in space, but only the registration of a movement which will be erased and rewritten." The extract is taken from Antonino Saggio, *Peter Eisenman. Trivellazioni nel futuro*, Testo & Immagine, Torino 1996. See also: Luca Galofaro, *Digital Eisenman. An Office of the Electronic Era*, Birkhäuser, Basel 1999 [Italian edition: *Eisenman digitale. Uno studio dell'era elettronica*, Testo & Immagine, Torino 1999].

2.6 A Visceral Nature

In "Multiplicitous and In-organic Bodies" (*AD profile* no. 106, 1993), Lynn writes: "In 1917 the researcher on morphogenesis D'Arcy Thompson described the transformation of natural forms in response to environmental forces [...]. The spatial organism is no longer seen as a static unit separated from external forces, but instead a sensitive system in continuous transformation through the interiorisation of external events [...]. The introduction into architecture of 'protogeometric' forms, namely with no exact measurement, opens up this possibility [...]. This is completely different from anthropomorphism where the body becomes a connection between nature and architecture through the proportional and geometric correspondence of the part to the whole." See also: Greg Lynn, "Architectural Curvilinearity: the Fold, the Pliant and the Supple", in *AD*, n. 102, 1993.

In "The New Canvas" (*AD profile*, no. 136, 1998), Frazer and Rastogi write: "While there have been other changes in the concept of space compared to the rigid mathematical and conceptualised space of the 15th and 16th centuries [...], today's change is fundamental, marking the transition from a static model to an evolutional biological model [...]. The new techniques of computerised design model the internal logic more than the external form." See also: John Frazer, *Evolutionary Architecture*, Academy Editions, London 1995. On Gehry and for further bibliographic references: Antonino Saggio, *Frank O. Gehry. Architetture residuali*, Testo & Immagine, Torino 1997.

2.7 Virtuality
By Markos Novak, "Transarchitecture and Hypersuface", in *Il progetto*, no. 3, 1998; *Architectural Design*, no. 136, 1998.

2.8 Sensitivity
In addition to Brand 93, by Nicholas Negroponte, *The Architecture Machine*, MIT Press, Cambridge 1970; *Soft Machine Architecture*, MIT Press, Cambridge 1975; *Being Digital*, Knopf, New York 1995. For a dossier on the elimination of architectural barriers, see the site http://casaccia.enea.it/andi/casa.htm. On the Nox Architects, see *Architectural Design*, no. 133 and no. 136, 1998.

3. THE LOGIC OF COMPLEXITY

3.1 Electronic Space
The idea of history as the gradual move away from the materiality of the place of origin (through the technical conquest of the elements earth, water, air) and the representation of the "alliance between technology and air" through the images of the embryo and the cosmonaut "divided from the mother, earth, matter", are taken from the book by Alessandro Boatto, *Della Guerra e dell'aria* (Costa & Nolan, Genoa 1992). Boatto's intriguing formula has been taken one step further through an additional dimensional leap: the figure of the cybernaut and its immersion in virtual reality appear to represent the tip of our current spatial dislocation. We also recall the fundamental contribution by Marc Augè who sees in the *excess of space*, the essential characteristic of *surmodernity*, a "moving away from ourselves that corresponds to the performance of cosmonauts and the endless rotation of our satellites" (M. Augé, *op.cit.*). On the overturning of the concept of nature and science brought about from the sixties onwards by the new theory of complexity, now aimed at the "possibility of a new science of the physis, a combined science of the non-living and the living" (Bocchi, Ceruti), in addition to the aforesaid works by Capra and Morin, see the collection of essays by Atlan, von Foerster, Lovelock, Morin, Prigogine, Varela, Zelany and others in: G. Bocchi and M. Ceruti (eds.), *La sfida della complessità*, Feltrinelli, Milano 1985 and 1991. Marcello Cini, *Un paradiso perduto*, Feltrinelli, Milano 1994.

3.2 The Corporeal Machine
On interactivity and architecture, see the postface by Antonino Saggio "Hyperarchitettura", in Prestinenza 98 and "Interactivity", in Maria Rita Perbellini

The Information Technology Revolution in Architecture is a new series reflecting on the effects the virtual dimension is having on architects and architecture in general. Each volume will examine a single topic, highlighting the essential aspects and exploring their relevance for the architects of today.

Series edited by **Antonino Saggio**

Other titles in this series:

Information Architecture
Basis and future of CAAD
Gerhard Schmitt
ISBN 3-7643-6092-5

HyperArchitecture
Spaces in the Electronic Age
Luigi Prestinenza Puglisi
ISBN 3-7643-6093-3

Digital Eisenman
An Office of the Electronic Era
Luca Galofaro
ISBN 3-7643-6094-1

Digital Stories
The Poetics of Communication
Maia Engeli
ISBN 3-7643-6175-1

Virtual Terragni
Young American Architects
Christian Pongratz / Maria Rita Perbellini
ISBN 3-7643-6174-3

Natural Born CAADesigners
Young American Architects
Christian Pongratz / Maria Rita Perbellini
ISBN 3-7643-6246-4

New Flatness
Surface Tension in Digital Architecture
Alicia Imperiale
ISBN 3-7643-6295-2

Digital Design
New Frontiers for the Objects
Paolo Martegani / Riccardo Montenegro
ISBN 3-7643-6296-0

For our free catalog please contact:

Birkhäuser – Publishers for Architecture
P. O. Box 133, CH-4010 Basel, Switzerland
Tel. ++41-(0)61-205 07 07; Fax ++41-(0)61-205 07 92
e-mail: sales@birkhauser.ch
http://www.birkhauser.ch